W9-ADK-902

*Children with Exceptional
Needs in Regular
Classrooms*

The Advisory Panel

Judith McIntosh Bell, Interrelated Teacher, Adrian Elementary School, Georgia

Glenna Clark, New Directions Program, Saxe Middle School, Special Education Department, New Canaan, Connecticut

John Delonas, Learning Consultant, Blairstown Elementary School, New Jersey

Eugene Kroschel, School Social Worker, New Trier High School, Winnetka, Illinois

Alexandra Jaworski Prober, Teacher/Writer, Altadena, California

Children with Exceptional Needs in Regular Classrooms

Libby G. Cohen, Editor

nea PROFESSIONAL LIBRARY

National Education Association
Washington, D.C.

Copyright © 1992
National Education Association of the United States

Printing History
  First Printing: January 1992
  Second Printing: September 1993

Note

The opinions expressed in this publication should not be construed as representing the policy or position of the National Education Association. Materials published by the NEA Professional Library are intended to be discussion documents for teachers who are concerned with specialized interests of the profession.

Library of Congress Cataloging-in-Publication Data

Children with exceptional needs in regular classrooms / Libby G.
    Cohen, editor.
        p.   cm.—(Aspects of learning)
    Includes bibliographical references.
    "Stock no. 3009500"—Cover.
    ISBN 0-8106-3009-5
    1. Special education—United States. 2. Mainstreaming in
education—United States.   I. Cohen, Libby G.   II. Series.
LC3981.C48   1992
371.9'046'0973—dc20   20   90-25366
                                                                  CIP

371.9046
G 53

93.2611
22862445

CONTENTS

PREFACE, by Libby G. Cohen   7

CHAPTER 1.   CLASSROOM MANAGEMENT
STRATEGIES FOR STUDENTS WITH
BEHAVIOR DISORDERS
by Raymond M. Glass 11

CHAPTER 2.   TEACHING ELEMENTARY SCHOOL
CHILDREN WITH MILD SPECIAL
NEEDS IN THE REGULAR CLASSROOM
by Charles M. Lyons 37

CHAPTER 3.   ASSESSING STUDENTS WITH SPECIAL
NEEDS: CURRENT AND EMERGING
PERSPECTIVES
by Libby G. Cohen 48

CHAPTER 4.   STUDENTS WITH MILD HANDICAPS
IN SECONDARY CLASSROOMS
by Jo Anna Spruill 63

CHAPTER 5.   MAINSTREAMING THE CHILD
WITH A VISUAL IMPAIRMENT
by Loraine J. Spenciner 82

CHAPTER 6.   STUDENTS WITH HEARING
IMPAIRMENTS
by Toni Rees 98

CHAPTER 7.   TEACHING STUDENTS WITH SEVERE
             DISABILITIES IN THE REGULAR
             CLASSROOM
             by Joanne W. Putnam 118

CHAPTER 8.   GIFTED STUDENTS IN REGULAR
             CLASSROOMS
             by Susan B. Tarver and James A. Curry . 143

CHAPTER 9.   MICROCOMPUTER APPLICATIONS
             FOR TEACHING STUDENTS WITH
             EXCEPTIONAL NEEDS IN THE
             REGULAR CLASSROOM
             by Berttram Chiang 163

THE CONTRIBUTORS 182

PREFACE

The acceleration of change compels us to perceive life as motion, not as order; the universe not as complete, but as unfinished. (4, p. 20)*

John F. Kennedy relished telling the following story about Marshal Lyautey, a famous French soldier:

> Upon meeting his gardener, Marshal Lyautey instructed him to plant a rare variety of trees in his garden the next day. The gardener replied that he would be happy to do as he had been told but that it would take 100 years for the trees to mature. On hearing the gardener's response, the Marshal told him to plant the trees that afternoon. (2)

In this anecdote, the future seems to be far away. What difference can a day make? Yet there is an urgency. Every day is important, and even more so when we think of the days that children spend in school. Changes in the education of children with exceptional needs are occurring before our eyes. The pace of change forces us to see education as in motion (4). This book links the recent changes that have taken place in the education of students with exceptional needs with the results of research and with preferred instructional strategies.

Over the past three decades, much progress and many changes have occurred in the education of students with exceptional needs in regular classrooms. During the 1960s educators and parents, influenced by the civil rights movement, began to realize that children with handicaps had a right to participate in education in public schools, that these children did not have to be segregated and isolated.

---

*Numbers in parentheses appearing in the text refer to the References at the end of the chapter.

In 1975, the Education for All Handicapped Children Act (P.L. 94–142) was passed. This landmark law provided that all children who were handicapped were entitled to a free, appropriate public education and that this education should be delivered in the least restrictive environment. During the late 1980s and early 1990s, the momentum for change has increased. Started in 1986, the Regular Education Initiative (REI) has become a movement that is pressing for additional accommodation of children with handicaps in regular schools and classrooms. We have realized that more has to be done and that there should be an increased emphasis on delivery of instructional services to these children in regular classrooms.

While some writers (3, 5) have strongly urged that all students be educated in regular classrooms, others (1) have cautioned that we need to think carefully about how all children can be included in regular classrooms and schools. A reconceptualization is thus emerging over how all students can be accommodated in this way.

Research conducted during the past few decades has yielded rich results (6, 7). While we have much to learn about teaching children who are exceptional, there is much that we do know. And, while the debate continues over the extent to which special education and regular education should merge and over the form that it should take, it is evident that regular classroom teachers are expected to accommodate students with special needs in their classrooms.

The contributors to this book discuss how these children can be accommodated in regular classrooms. In particular, they examine

- the characteristics of children with exceptional needs
- how students with exceptional needs can be accommodated in regular classrooms
- effective instructional strategies to use with these students

8

- the legal requirements for educating students with special needs
- strategies that can be used to evaluate classroom performance.

The book explores three themes. The contributors have reflected upon the changes that have occurred in the education of students who are exceptional, and they have considered the legal requirements in educating these students. And relying on the results of research, they discuss emerging trends and preferred practices for teaching these students in regular classrooms.

The publication of this book would not have been possible without the hard work of a number of people. Each contributor has my deep gratitude and respect. In addition, Rebecca Smith and Pearl Wuthrich have provided invaluable assistance. Finally, Les and Seth continue to offer their sense of humor and encouragement for which I am deeply appreciative.

—Libby G. Cohen

REFERENCES

1. Bellamy, T. "School Reform for All Students: An Essay Review of *Beyond Separate Education: Quality Education for All*." *Journal of the Association for Persons with Severe Handicaps* 14, no. 3 (Fall 1989): 241–45.
2. Hofstadter, D. R. *Metamagical Themas: Questing for the Essence of Mind and Pattern*. New York: Bantam, 1986.
3. Lipsky, D. K., and Gartner, A. *Beyond Separate Education*. Baltimore: Paul H. Brookes, 1989.
4. Schlesinger, A., Jr. "The Challenge of Change." *New York Times Magazine*, July 27, 1986: 20–22.
5. Stainback, S.; Stainback, W.; and Forest, M. *Educating All Students in the Mainstream of Regular Education*. Baltimore: Paul H. Brookes, 1989.

6. Wang, M. C.; Reynolds, M. C.; and Walberg, H. J. *Handbook of Special Education, Vol. 1.* Oxford, England: Pergamon, 1987.
7. _____. *Handbook of Special Education, Vol. 2.* Oxford, England: Pergamon, 1988.

Chapter 1

CLASSROOM MANAGEMENT STRATEGIES FOR STUDENTS WITH BEHAVIOR DISORDERS

by Raymond M. Glass

Raymond Glass begins our consideration of students with exceptional needs with a discussion of classroom management strategies. He considers three main themes. The first theme focuses on preventive strategies; it is based on the assumption that it is usually more efficient to prevent problems from developing than it is to devote instructional time to their resolution. The second theme explores specific teacher strategies to employ when preventive measures do not eliminate misbehavior. The third theme looks at strategies to build self-control and develop more appropriate social skills.

There is little doubt that student misbehavior concerns most teachers. Few educators have not been faced with occasional misbehavior in the form of defiance, excessive talking out of turn, refusal to complete work, or fighting, and many face chronic misbehavior from one or more children on a daily basis. Indeed, in an NEA teacher survey conducted in 1984 as many as 45 percent of the respondents reported that student misbehavior interfered with their teaching to either a great or a moderate degree. The problem of how best to respond to misbehavior may be compounded if the student is already labeled behavior disordered, emotionally disturbed, learning disabled, or developmentally delayed. Such labels may cause teachers to question their own training and expertise when it comes to providing appropriate classroom management for these mainstreamed students.

This chapter examines a variety of classroom management strategies for use with students who have behavior problems. The strategies will be appropriate for a wide range of students, from those who demonstrate relatively mild misbehavior to those with more frequent and/or serious problems. The chapter is divided into three main sections. The first section focuses on specific classroom management strategies designed to prevent problems, as it is nearly always more effective to prevent problems than to devote instructional time to their resolution. The second section explores specific strategies to help students improve their classroom behavior and addresses the question of what to do when preventive measures alone fail to quell misbehavior. And since the goal of classroom management is not only to prevent misbehavior but also to teach students self-control and constructive interaction skills, the final section is devoted to these concerns.

PREVENTING BEHAVIOR PROBLEMS— THE WELL-MANAGED CLASSROOM

Almost two decades ago Jere Brophy and Carolyn Evertson, two well-known students of classroom management and student achievement, concluded that classroom management skills are of primary importance in determining teaching success (1). Indeed, it is generally understood that students who display mild to moderate forms of behavior problems often perform much better in classrooms that are well managed. Conversely, these same students demonstrate higher levels of off-task behavior in poorly managed classrooms (7, 18). Thus, much problem behavior can be averted through careful classroom management procedures such as those described in the following pages.

Establish Clear Rules and Procedures

Central to any effort to prevent problem behavior is the establishment of clear rules and procedures. Rules typically refer to standards for student behavior, such as "Raise your hand before talking" or "Work quietly during seatwork time." Procedures refer to a variety of conventions to help the class run smoothly; they may include explicit guidelines such as what to do when finished with seatwork, how to get help when the teacher is engaged with other students, what to do upon entering the classroom at the beginning of a period, and where to put completed assignments.

The importance of clear rules and procedures can be underrated because many teachers who experience high levels of disruptive behavior believe they have clear rules and procedures. In their comparison of well- and poorly managed elementary and junior high school classrooms, however, Evertson and Emmer (7) found that the successful classroom managers described their rules with greater clarity, stated desired behaviors and expectations more often, praised students for following rules more frequently, and pointed out infractions more quickly than their less successful colleagues. In short, these successful classroom managers devoted more time at the beginning of the school year to describe, review, rehearse, and reward appropriate student behavior, an investment that obviously had a high rate of return in terms of student behavior and learning.

Maintain Momentum

Successful classroom managers demonstrate more than clear rules and procedures. They also employ constructive ways to gain and maintain student attention and handle minor disruptions in an unobtrusive manner (16). That is, they initiate lessons and keep them moving forward with a minimum of interruptions; when they do respond to misbehavior, it is often in a calm, firm manner that allows the class to get back to the lesson

13

quickly (18). A variety of momentum-maintaining strategies are described by Jones and Jones (16), Kounin (18), and Saphier and Gower (21). Descriptions of several of these strategies follow.

- Develop signals to indicate when students are to give you their full attention. Common signals include the teacher raising a hand, ringing a bell, or turning off the lights. Effectively used, such signals allow teachers to gain student attention quickly and quietly.

- Ensure smooth lessons by having all materials ready at the beginning of the class, developing routines for passing out and collecting materials, and checking for student understanding before assigning seatwork. These procedures are particularly important for students with behavior disorders who tend to become anxious and disruptive when confused about work they are to do.

- Call on students randomly during drill or question-and-answer sessions, rather than first stating a name and then directing the question to the named student. In addition, consider the use of choral responding and fast-paced questions and answers during drill activities. Such strategies tend to keep students alert and in tune with the activity.

- Convey your awareness of what students are doing. Relatively easy ways to convey awareness include frequent scanning of the class, circulating around the classroom, and using a seating arrangement that allows you to view all students.

- Reinforce potential problem students for remembering to follow rules and allude to the contributions of these and other students during discussions. Such techniques often help to secure and maintain involvement with the lesson.

- Develop several unobtrusive "first responses" to minor misbehaviors such as talking out of turn. Some of these responses include standing near the student, conveying a nonverbal message such as placing a finger on the lips or pointing to a posted rule, or quietly reminding the student of the rule or the consequences for not following the rule. The critical point to remember is to respond to the student in a manner that does not interrupt the momentum of the lesson.
- Develop individualized responses to students. For some students, momentary frustration with tasks can initiate anxiety. Not knowing how to begin a task, or feeling stuck or overwhelmed may lead to minor misbehavior. Many students with behavior disorders may require additional explanations, help doing the first one or two seatwork problems, or the availability of a "buddy" or well-behaved student who can provide limited help as needed. Others may need to be firmly reminded of consequences of their misbehavior.

Use Effective Communication Skills

Students with behavior disorders often create in teachers the same feelings of anger and frustration they themselves experience. In a few short seconds we may find ourselves feeling threatened and responding to students with ultimatums. In the worst cases, angry outbursts may occur between teacher and student that may create anxiety for other students. The following dialogue between Mr. Wing and Bob, a mainstreamed student with behavior disorders, illustrates how Mr. Wing avoids a confrontation by recognizing Bob's feelings, avoiding threats, and helping Bob begin his work.

Mr. Wing: All right class, let's try some practice problems. We've done the first three together and I want you to do the next five by yourself.

15

Bob: (Feeling fearful of working alone) I hate to do these problems. I can't see why we have to do these, they're stupid. I'm skipping them.

Mr. Wing: (Speaking privately and recognizing Bob's anxiety about working alone) Bob, what's up?

Bob: (Plaintively) I hate this kind of work. Do I have to do it?

Mr. Wing: Sounds like you're not feeling too sure about whether you can do these alone.

Bob: (Looking sheepish) Yeah.

Mr. Wing: What did you do yesterday when you had to work alone?

Bob: I did one at a time.

Mr. Wing: Right! How about trying that today? Do the first two and then call me over.

While not all potential confrontations are so smoothly averted, it is important to keep in mind that confrontations between teacher and student often create an emotionally charged atmosphere that is detrimental to learning. Responding to students in a calm, supportive manner that recognizes student feelings or concerns will go a long way toward minimizing disruptions and building trust between teacher and student.

Use Formal Discipline Programs

In addition to the preceding strategies, some teachers find it useful to employ a formal classroom discipline program such as Assertive Discipline, developed by Lee and Marlene Canter (3). Teachers using Assertive Discipline typically develop and post four to six classroom rules; then they clearly state the rewards and consequences for compliance or noncompliance with the rules, as indicated in Figure 1.

Central to this approach is a teacher who responds to students in a firm, businesslike manner. Thus, when applying checkmarks or otherwise enforcing rules, teachers are encouraged to avoid negotiating or debating infractions. Instead, the teacher writes a checkmark and continues with the lesson. A typical

Figure 1
Typical Rules and Consequences
Used in Assertive Discipline

CLASS RULES
1. Raise your hand before talking.
2. Work quietly.
3. Be polite. Follow the teacher's directions.
4. Be respectful. Listen carefully and speak to others politely.
5. Walk quietly about the room and school.

CONSEQUENCES
1. First infraction = Warning
2. Second infraction = Name on board—loss of 15 minutes of recess
3. Third infraction = Checkmark next to name and 20 minutes after school
4. Fourth infraction = Checkmark next to name and immediate phone call to parent. May result in removal from the class for the day.

REWARDS
When everyone is working hard and following the rules, a marble will be dropped in a jar. When the class earns 100 marbles, we will earn a 20-minute activity period.

---

strategy for applying consequences is to put a student's name on the board for a first rule infraction (e.g., talking out of turn, or not getting to work on time), with checkmarks added for subsequent infractions of any rule.

While consequences are administered to individuals, rewards for compliance with the rules are earned by all class members. For example, a teacher might award the class a point or drop a marble in a jar when everyone has followed the rules for the first half of a class period. A class reward such as a movie, a story, a popcorn party, or an extra recess is earned when a predetermined number of points or marbles is reached.

Some writers such as Jones and Jones (16) and Curwin and Mendler (4) are skeptical of Assertive Discipline, claiming that there is relatively little solid research to support the program. In addition, these authors believe that Assertive Discipline demands compliance but does not help students develop self-control and problem-solving skills. These are serious considerations; the teacher who employs Assertive Discipline should keep these limitations in mind. The final section of this chapter reviews several approaches to helping students develop self-control and problem-solving skills.

BEYOND PREVENTION—HELPING STUDENTS IMPROVE THEIR BEHAVIOR

Even the most skillful application of preventive techniques will not eliminate all problem behavior, and it is likely that at least one or two students in almost any classroom may require more concerted efforts than those just described. This section explores frameworks to help us understand why students may engage in persistent misbehavior. Then it considers several approaches to managing such misbehavior.

Why Students Misbehave

Having some understanding of why students misbehave can help us cope with difficult students and plan long-term strategies for working with them. Fortunately, there are several complementary frameworks for understanding misbehavior that many teachers find useful; brief descriptions of these follow.

Dreikurs' Four Goals of Misbehavior

Rudolf Dreikurs and his colleagues (6) suggest that a small percentage of students find it difficult to meet their needs for recognition and approval through appropriate school behavior and may misbehave to accomplish goals of attention, control, revenge, or withdrawal.

We can determine a student's goal of misbehavior by observing the behavior as well as our own reactions to the student. For example, *attention-oriented* students often misbehave to gain recognition from adults even if the recognition is less than positive. These students may talk out of turn, continually ask for help, or make inappropriate comments. Frequently we respond to their misbehavior by giving them attention in the form of reprimands because we may feel annoyed and frustrated with their constant interruptions. This inadvertent attention can reinforce the misbehavior.

Control-oriented students often refuse our requests and defy our authority. They may view defiance of our requests as a way of asserting their own power, and frequently engage us in what Dreikurs refers to as a "battle of the wills." These students often make us feel threatened and angry, and a natural response may be to try to force the student to comply with our requests. While such efforts may occasionally work, they often simply escalate the battle of the wills and result in angry confrontations.

Revenge-oriented students are less concerned with attention or control. Instead, their goal is to inflict emotional or physical pain on others through put-downs, name-calling, or defacing property. The fundamental perspective of revenge-oriented students is that they feel pain and anger in themselves, which they in turn create in others through their behaviors. Not surprisingly, revenge-oriented students often make teachers feel hurt, and they may respond to these students with threats, sarcasm, or anger. Such responses may confirm the student's belief that revengeful behavior is acceptable and common.

The final goal of misbehavior is *withdrawal* or *assumed disability*. Students with this goal have given up on school or specific subjects, believing they can't learn, and they develop an implicit contract with many teachers that states, "Don't expect anything from me and I won't bother you." Assumed-disability students may passively resist our efforts to engage them in learning based on their belief that they are incapable.

19

Dreikurs cautions us to examine our own feelings and reactions to students who display the four behavior patterns described and to try to avoid falling into the following vicious cycles: (1) constantly responding to the inappropriate behavior of the attention getter; (2) engaging in confrontations and battles of the will with the control-oriented; (3) responding to the revenge-oriented with sarcasm or punitiveness; and (4) giving up on the assumed-disability student.

Kohlberg's Stages of Moral Development

A second useful framework for understanding misbehavior is provided by Lawrence Kohlberg (17), whose stage theory of moral development builds on the work of Jean Piaget (20). Like Piaget, Kohlberg views moral development as a gradual unfolding process beginning with the *premoral* child whose conduct is guided more by the fear of punishment or the prospect of obtaining rewards or pleasure than by an inner sense of what is morally appropriate or helpful. In school, such children follow rules and procedures to avoid punishment or receive rewards or favors. Students typically move on to the *conventional* level of moral development where they may look to peers and significant authority figures to guide their conduct. Thus, conventional-level students may observe rules and procedures to avoid censure or to win the respect of peers and significant others. The highest level of moral development involves the establishment of an internalized set of ethics or beliefs. At this stage, students are able to clearly articulate rather complex reasons for making decisions involving moral principles.

Although Kohlberg's stage theory of moral development is not universally accepted by developmental psychologists, the framework may help teachers to develop appropriate management strategies for difficult children. For example, premoral students can be found at any age level and need very clear rules and limits; they usually profit from rewards for behaving appropriately and completing work on time. These same students may misbehave when the learning activity is ambiguous or when the rules for behavior have not been clearly spelled out. In describing their efforts with students at the premoral level, many teachers say they have to spell out exactly what they want a student to do, when it is to be done, what the reward will be for completing the task, and what the consequences will be for misbehavior.

Kohlberg's framework also cautions us regarding the use of an overly restrictive classroom management program if we are to help students move to higher levels of moral development. Teachers who are too controlling may reinforce their authority and gain student compliance but may not establish conditions that promote student problem solving and further moral development. This concern is quite similar to the argument against Assertive Discipline put forth by Curwin and Mendler (5). Indeed, Assertive Discipline may be very useful with students at the premoral level as an effective means of making rewards and consequences crystal clear. Once a reasonable measure of student compliance is obtained, however, the program should be abandoned or altered significantly to help students learn problem-solving skills.

Biophysical Considerations

A final framework looks at misbehavior from a biophysical perspective; it recognizes that some student misbehavior may be caused by physiological problems. Students with various forms of seizure activity as well as those who are hyperactive would fit into this category. Of late, there has been an increase in the number of students labeled as having attention-deficit disorders (2), and it is generally believed that such students have minimal central nervous system damage that makes it difficult for them to focus their attention. Many of these students are also overactive or hyperactive, which makes it difficult for them to remain still for long periods of time or to exercise complete fine motor control.

While not all student misbehavior can be explained by the three frameworks just reviewed, these and similar frameworks can help us better understand and respond to student misbehavior. The following pages examine specific management strategies teachers have found useful in their work with students who meet many of the behavior patterns just described.

Strategies for Managing Misbehavior

The author has conducted numerous workshops and training programs with classroom teachers to identify effective strategies for students whose misbehavior could be explained by one or more of the frameworks identified. The following list is based on ideas from classroom teachers; students of behavior management such as Jones and Jones (16), Wolfgang and Glickman (24), and Dreikurs, Grunwald, and Pepper (6); and the author's own experience as a teacher and consultant. Although the list focuses on responses to attention-, control-, revenge-, and withdrawal-oriented students, many strategies also apply to students with attention-deficit problems and hyperactivity, as well as to those at the premoral level of development.

For attention-oriented students:
- Give these students your attention when they are behaving appropriately. "Catch them being good" and give them praise or recognition during these moments.
- Find ways to give students recognition through legitimate classroom responsibilities and jobs.
- When students talk too often or ask too many questions, ask them privately to identify how many times they will need to talk out or request help during a given lesson or time period. Then, ask them to keep track. Praise these students for keeping within their established quotas and then encourage them to decrease the quota.
- Provide primary grade children with a limited number

of chips or tokens for a certain behavior, such as asking a question or talking out. Each time the student engages in the behavior, he or she gives a chip to the teacher. The chips serve as a concrete reminder to limit certain behaviors.

- Avoid responding to attention-getting students engaging in mild forms of misbehavior, whenever possible. Instead, praise or recognize other students for their helpful behavior.
- Seek out a moment or two each day just to relate to the student. This will help some students understand that you are interested in them as individuals and that they may not have to engage in inappropriate behavior to gain your attention.
- Anticipate the needs of attention-oriented students and include them in the lesson. For example, if you know that a student enjoys making humorous comments at the beginning of seatwork activities, ask the student if there is anything he or she would like to say or contribute that may make everyone laugh.

For control-oriented students:
- Avoid arguments. As Dreikurs warns, we need to take the "sails out of the wind" of control-oriented students. Such students cannot win a battle if we simply choose to walk away from the potential confrontation.
- Give reasonable choices. Allow some choice in what assignments need to be done (e.g., "You may do any five of the ten problems."), where the work is to be done (e.g., "You may work at your desk or at a worktable."), or how the work is to be done (e.g., "You may work alone or with a partner).
- Find ways to give legitimate control and responsibility to these students. Make them line leaders or tutors for

younger students.

- Use a "broken record" technique for students who continually challenge the rules. Without getting angry, simply restate the rules or procedures, giving no other explanations. Repeat this each time the student challenges.
- Control the times you will engage in debate with a student. If the student is getting argumentative about an assignment or a grade, end the discussion by telling her/him you cannot take time now to talk but that you can be available later.
- Establish and maintain clear limits and consequences. For example, incomplete work must be made up after school, during recess, or at home. Carry out consequences or limits in a calm, matter-of-fact manner using additional techniques such as the broken record.
- Develop contracts. Meet with a student privately and negotiate the specific behaviors you want to see each day, as well as the amount and quality of work you expect on a daily or weekly basis. Specify rewards and consequences for meeting or not meeting the conditions of the contract. Encourage the student to help you formulate each aspect of the contract to promote a spirit of working together.

For revenge-oriented students:

- Understand the revenge-oriented student's basic mistrust and anger toward others as well as the need to hurt others through put-downs and other acts.
- Relate to the student with respect and encouragement when the student demonstrates appropriate academic or social behavior.
- Attempt to build the student's self-esteem by recognizing and promoting positive abilities and skills.
- Realize that revenge-oriented students may be wary of

relationships. Understand their need for distance and do not overpraise.

- Respond to revenge-oriented behavior in a calm manner. Avoid making threats and giving out punishments on the spur of the moment. Instead, develop a clear set of consequences for certain misbehaviors before they occur and carry them out firmly, but calmly, indicating that hurting others cannot be tolerated. Do not carry a grudge, and try to begin the next day or class period with a clean slate.
- Give more attention to the injured student, verbalizing out loud that students sometimes hurt others because they feel hurt and upset.

For withdrawal-oriented or assumed-disability students:
- Maintain your enthusiasm and belief that the student can learn even though the student may insist that he or she is unable to learn.
- Encourage and reward small bits of improvement.
- Employ games, contracts, progress charts, and other motivational devices to keep learning exciting.
- Encourage the student to demonstrate his or her knowledge by using oral reports and other vehicles that do not require high levels of reading, writing, or math skills. Try to increase the student's level of involvement in all activities by building on strengths.
- Remember that assumed-disability students believe they can't learn and often convince other adults. Avoid becoming discouraged and giving up on the student.

Each of these strategies has proven useful for different teachers because it provided a way to avoid falling into the vicious cycles described earlier.

Systematic Reward Programs

Despite the value of the strategies just reviewed, a few students with problem behavior may require more systematic approaches such as those provided by structured reward programs. The following pages review several programs that regular classroom teachers can readily apply to improve the behavior of individual students.

Systematic Feedback

Feedback or knowledge of one's performance can be a powerful motivator. Many students who are somewhat aware of their misbehavior and who can understand specific objectives established for them (e.g., "Finish at least 10 math problems during a math period." "Talk out of turn no more than twice per discussion period.") are often interested in knowing how well they performed these objectives. Thus, we can tell students how they performed a range of behaviors, such as how many words they spelled correctly, how many math problems they completed in a given time period, or how often they remembered to raise their hand before talking. We can provide this feedback by keeping a tally of a particular behavior and then telling the student at the end of a class period how he or she performed. This information can then be recorded on a chart, graph, or other device so the student's performance over several days or weeks can be viewed and compared.

Another form of feedback is a good behavior chart or checklist that is completed by the teacher or by the teacher and student. Charts such as the one presented in Figure 2 list the key behaviors the teacher is trying to promote as well as a rating indicating how well the student performed each objective. Good behavior charts can be reviewed at logical points such as the end of a class period or morning. The teacher may spend a brief moment reviewing the behaviors with the student and then enter the appropriate codes on the chart.

Figure 2

Good Behavior Chart

Student _____ Date _____

1. I completed my reading seatwork by 10:15.   _____
2. I stayed in my seat during seatwork time (9:30–   _____
   10:15
3. I lined up for recess without pushing, running, or _____
   hitting.
4. I raised my hand before talking during science or   _____
   social studies.

Key: 3 = Excellent work! All tasks or behaviors were com-
          pleted. No teacher reminders were needed.
      2 = OK. Most work was done or the behaviors were
          followed most of the time. A few reminders were
          needed.
      0 = Needs improvement. Only some of the work was
          done or the behaviors were followed only some of the
          time. More than six reminders were needed.

Students can take increasing responsibility for completing charts as their skill and motivation improve. At the beginning
of a feedback or charting program, the teacher may complete all
ratings or information to ensure consistency and accuracy.
Students can gradually take an increasing role in this process
until, finally, they rate their own behavior with the teacher
endorsing the student's self-rating. The use of student self-rating
has been found to be a powerful tool in helping students improve
their behavior at both the elementary and the junior high school
levels (19, 23).

Rewarding Positive Behavior

While feedback alone may be a strong enough motivator
to improve student behavior, additional incentives often need to

be applied. Certainly a logical place to start is by providing warm praise and encouragement to the student for appropriate behavior as you are completing a good behavior chart or other feedback device. Additional incentives such as special privileges may also prove helpful. For example, a student might earn a privilege such as computer time, 10 minutes to play a game with a friend, or a library pass for demonstrating appropriate behavior.

Privileges should be awarded according to a carefully designed plan. First, the teacher identifies specific behaviors the student should demonstrate or reduce; then the teacher discusses these as well as possible privileges privately with the student so that a clear agreement or contract is developed ("After your spelling is completed you may listen to a record." "If you earn 15 points on your daily report card, you may play a game for 10 minutes at the end of class."). As a general rule, privileges should be offered as soon as possible after the desired behavior occurs, which is usually at the end of a class period or at the end of a morning or day. As students achieve success with a privilege program, they may work for more long-term rewards, such as a special activity period or field trip.

Coordinating Reward Programs
with Parents and Special Educators

Whenever possible, feedback and reward programs should be coordinated with special education personnel and parents. Special educators may add valuable insight into which behaviors should be identified for improvement and may also be able to provide additional coaching, support, and incentives to help the student perform these behaviors. In addition, special educators may be in a position to provide certain rewards and privileges—such as time to watch a video, or a bag of popcorn—that would prove disruptive in a large classroom. Thus, in some cases, a completed good behavior checklist may be sent to the special educator on a daily basis with that teacher also reviewing the chart and providing the reward.

Good behavior charts such as the one shown in Figure 2 can be easily adapted for use as daily home-school notes, which may have a powerful impact on student behavior (13). To initiate a home-school note program, a phone call or a conference with the parent should be conducted to determine whether the parent is interested in receiving daily feedback. Assuming there is parental interest, specific procedures should be clarified such as how often the note is to be sent home, what the parent should do if the note is not received, and what types of incentives should be used. The author's experience suggests that these programs often generate an immediate improvement in student behavior, provided the teacher is consistent in sending the note home and the parent is consistent in applying rewards. Rewards can come in the form of an allowance program, with each point earned having a monetary value such as four or five cents, or a daily or weekly privilege program. For example, the student may earn nightly TV time or a weekly trip to a fast-food restaurant by earning a predetermined number of points at school.

Home-school incentive programs are not always successful. They will have little, if any, impact on student behavior if the parent is not interested or does not follow through on a regular basis. Moreover, caution is indicated if there is suspicion that the student comes from an abusive home, because the parent may use less-than-perfect notes as an excuse to punish the student.

PROMOTING PROBLEM SOLVING AND ACTIVE PARTICIPATION—MOVING FROM COMPLIANCE TO COOPERATION

Thus far we have examined strategies designed to understand and contain student misbehavior. For example, we can minimize the impact of the control-oriented student by avoiding unnecessary battles of the will, providing some choice and opportunities for responsibility, and, if necessary, designing a reward and/or home-school incentive program. While these strategies can be quite effective, they are limited in that they are designed to bring about compliance without teaching students important new problem-solving and social skills. This section examines several strategies designed to develop these critical skills.

Developing Problem-Solving Skills

William Glasser (10, 11) asserts that students need to experience a sense of responsibility and involvement in solving problems and that teachers who simply administer rewards and punishments may deny students valuable learning experiences. To accomplish this sense of responsibility and involvement, Glasser proposes that teachers engage misbehaving students in dialogues that follow a procedure in which the teacher (1) meets privately with the student to discuss, in a supportive manner, the misbehavior that has occurred; (2) asks the student to identify the misbehavior and then consider how the behavior is affecting the student or class; (3) helps the student work out a specific plan regarding more constructive behaviors the student will employ when similar situations arise; (4) develops with the student a set of rewards or consequences for enacting or failing to enact the plan; and (5) reviews the plan periodically, revising it as needed with the student's assistance.

Teachers who have successfully used this technique do not conduct a problem-solving conference when the student is upset, but, instead, wait for a more appropriate time. In addition, they do not accept general plans, such as "Next time I'll do better." Rather, they insist on specific details—such as "Next time I get frustrated, I will raise my hand for help instead of crumpling up my paper and throwing it."—and then carefully monitor student progress.

Glasser advocates a similar procedure for teaching problem solving to the entire class through classroom meetings that are designed to solve everyday problems affecting the groups. Once a problem is identified and understood, suggestions from students are solicited and discussed, with the teacher and class arriving at an agreeable solution. Typical problems for classroom meetings may involve how to cope with name-calling, how to use free time, how to give and get help, and how to deal constructively with frustration.

The entire class, as well as specific students with behavior problems, may also benefit from general training in solving interpersonal problems and using self-control. For example, students could be presented with common problems such as those listed in Figure 3. After a problem is described, students could be asked to identify and describe constructive solutions to the problem situations. Selected students can then be asked to demonstrate or role play these solutions.

As with any new skill, repeated practice is necessary, since many students will have had little or no experience with problem-solving techniques. Indeed, some students may initially respond in an impulsive or cavalier manner. Thus, classroom meetings and other forms of problem-solving activities need to be introduced frequently to help students learn the skills and apply them.

Developing Prosocial Skills

Closely related to problem-solving skills is the development of specific social and self-control skills. Many students with behavior problems lack specific skills, such as knowing how to share materials, to ignore the misbehavior of others, to cope with name-calling, to make an apology, or to accept help or constructive criticism, without getting upset. Often, it is the lack of these skills rather than poor academic performance that makes mainstreaming such students an uphill battle.

A relatively new area of focus is the development of social skills through direct instruction techniques of modeling, guided practice, reinforcement, and discussion (12, 14). For example, in the Jackson, Jackson, and Monroe program (14), the skill of handling name-calling and teasing is first carefully described by

31

Figure 3

Sample Discussion and Role-Playing Questions to Facilitate Problem Solving

- Everyone makes a difference in this class. Name something you said or did to make this a good class to be in.
- You are working on some math problems and are confused. You raise your hand for help but the teacher says she is busy and asks you to wait. What are two helpful things you can do?
- Your friend asks you to join a club. To get into the club, you have to steal something and bring it to a meeting. You don't want to steal. Describe how you would feel and demonstrate what you would say to your friend.
- You are walking across the room and someone trips you. You are not sure whether it was an accident. Demonstrate what you would say and do to avoid a fight.
- Joe and Sara are spelling partners and they want to help each other get a high score on the next test. Identify three ways they can help each other.
- Name a problem you are trying to solve and tell what you might do to solve the problem.
- You are working hard at your desk and the person behind you keeps kicking the back of your chair. Show a helpful way you would ask this person to stop.
- You accidentally knock something off someone's desk as you are walking by. Show what you would say and do to avoid angry feelings.
- Give an example of a time when you misbehaved to get attention from an adult.
- Give an example of a time when you did something that helped another adult.

From Glass, R., *Cooperation—A Game to Develop Social and Problem-Solving Skills Through Cooperative Learning Procedures* (Farmington: University of Maine at Farmington, Center for Cooperative Learning, 1989).

the teacher and then modeled through one or two demonstrations. To check for understanding, students are asked to identify the important behaviors demonstrated by the teacher. Guided practice is then provided through a series of brief role-playing episodes in which students must employ the skill. To promote transfer, students discuss the value of the skill, as well as alternative strategies if they employ the skill and it does not bring about satisfactory results (e.g., if a student tries to respond constructively to name-calling or teasing and continues to be the object of ridicule). In addition, students receive application assignments to try specific skills at home or in other situations at school. Finally, the teacher provides praise and other forms of reinforcement as students apply the various social skills.

The development of social and problem-solving skills will be greatly enhanced if students have an opportunity to put them into action on a daily basis. A powerful strategy for the development of both academic and social skills is to organize learning activities that require student interaction and cooperation (15, 22). In cooperative learning, students work together in small, heterogeneous groups to achieve a common academic goal such as the completion of a worksheet, assignment, or project. Cooperative learning groups can become a critical setting for students to practice and further develop a range of group participation and problem-solving skills. A detailed discussion of cooperative learning approaches appears in Chapter 7.

SUMMARY

It is clear that there is no formula for the instant resolution of problem behavior. However, it is suggested that three broad factors be considered when designing a management program for students with behavior problems. First, it is important to consider general classroom management approaches in an effort to prevent problem behavior from occurring. These efforts will influence all students and take into account the knowledge that students with behavior problems seem to function more effectively in clear, well-organized classrooms. A second factor extends beyond the well-managed classroom and focuses on developing frameworks for understanding and managing the problem behavior of specific students. The third factor suggests that teachers go beyond seeking compliance and help students develop social and problem-solving skills. Focusing on these three areas will bring benefits to all students, not just to those who are labeled exceptional.

DISCUSSION QUESTIONS

1. Describe a student who demonstrates behavior problems in your classroom. What does the student do? How does he or she make you feel? How do you typically respond? What impact do your responses have?
2. What additional strategies for attention-, control-, revenge-, or withdrawal-oriented students have you found useful?
3. What specific strategies do you use to help your students understand classroom rules and procedures? What areas might need further development?
4. Describe a daily feedback sheet or home-school procedures you have used with a difficult student or might now use.
5. Describe effective ways you have worked with a special educator or school psychologist to assist a student with behavior problems. What problems did you experience?

REFERENCES

1. Brophy, J., and Evertson, C. *Learning from Teaching: A Developmental Perspective.* Boston: Allyn and Bacon, 1976.
2. Campbell, S., and Werry, J. "Attention Deficit Disorder (Hyperactivity)." *Psychopathological Disorders of Childhood,* edited by H. Quay and J. Werry. 3d ed. New York: Wiley, 1986.

3. Canter, L. *Assertive Discipline.* Los Angeles: Lee Canter Associates, 1976.

4. Curwin, R., and Mendler, A. "Packaged Discipline Programs: Let the Buyer Beware." *Educational Leadership* 46, no. 2 (1988): 68–71.

5. _____. "We Repeat, Let the Buyer Beware: A Response to Canter." *Educational Leadership* 46, no. 6 (1989): 83.

6. Dreikurs, R.; Grunwald, B.; and Pepper, F. *Maintaining Sanity in the Classroom: Illustrated Teaching Techniques.* New York: Harper and Row, 1971.

7. Evertson, C., and Emmer, E. "Preventive Classroom Management." In *Helping Teachers Manage Classrooms,* edited by D. Duke. Alexandria, Va.: Association for Supervision and Curriculum Development, 1982.

8. Glass, R. "Planning and Organizing Instruction for Exceptional Children." In *Understanding Exceptional Children and Youth,* edited by P. Knoblock. Boston: Little, Brown and Company, 1987.

9. _____. *Cooperation: A Game to Develop Social and Problem-Solving Skills Through Cooperative Learning Procedures.* Farmington: University of Maine at Farmington, Center for Cooperative Learning, 1989.

10. Glasser, W. *Schools Without Failure.* New York: Harper and Row, 1969.

11. _____. *Control Theory: A New Explanation of How We Control Our Lives.* New York: Harper and Row, 1985.

12. Goldstein, A.; Sprafkin, R.; Gershaw, J.; and Klein, P. *Skillstreaming the Adolescent.* Champaign, Ill.: Research Press Company, 1980.

13. Imber, S.; Imber, R.; and Rothstein, C. "Modifying Independent Work Habits: An Effective Teacher-Parent Communication Program." *Exceptional Children* 46 (1979): 218–21.

14. Jackson, N.; Jackson, D.; and Monroe, C. *Getting Along with Others—Teaching Social Effectiveness to Children.* Champaign, Ill.: Research Press, 1983.

15. Johnson, D., and Johnson, R. "Mainstreaming and Cooperative Learning Strategies." *Exceptional Children* 52 (1986): 553–61.

16. Jones, V., and Jones, L. *Comprehensive Classroom Management.* 2d ed. Boston: Allyn and Bacon, 1986.

17. Kohlberg, L. "Moral Stages and Moralization: The Cognitive-Developmental Approach." In *Moral Development and Behavior,* edited by T. Lickona. New York: Holt, Rinehart, and Winston, 1976.
18. Kounin, J. *Discipline and Group Management in Classrooms.* New York: Holt, Rinehart, and Winston, 1970.
19. McLaughlin, T. "Effects of Self-Recording for On-Task and Academic Responding: A Long-Term Analysis." *Journal of Special Education Technology* 6 (1983): 5–11.
20. Piaget, J. *The Moral Judgment of the Child.* New York: Free Press, 1964.
21. Saphier, J., and Gower, R. *The Skillful Teacher.* Carlisle, Mass.: Research for Better Teaching, 1982.
22. Slavin, R. "Cooperative Learning and the Cooperative School." *Educational Leadership* 45, no. 3 (1987): 7–13.
23. Smith, D.; Young, R.; West, R.; Morgan, D.; and Rhode, G. "Reducing the Disruptive Behavior of Junior High Students: A Classroom Self-Management Procedure." *Behavior Disorders* 13 (1988): 213–39.
24. Wolfgang, C., and Glickman, C. *Solving Discipline Problems: Strategies for Classroom Teachers.* 2d ed. Boston: Allyn and Bacon, 1985.

Chapter 2

TEACHING ELEMENTARY SCHOOL CHILDREN WITH MILD SPECIAL NEEDS IN THE REGULAR CLASSROOM

by Charles M. Lyons

Charles Lyons points out that regular classroom teachers are closest to the child, and their importance in both planning and implementing programs for elementary-age students with mild handicaps is essential. Group management of children includes respect, caring, helping, establishing structure, and talking with students. Dr. Lyons discusses three processes that are critical in the development of sound classroom programs for serving these students: (1) defining the role of the classroom teacher on the child study team, (2) preparing a regular classroom for teaching students with special needs, and (3) managing learning in diverse groups.

If it is true that good group pedagogical techniques are truly functions of the entire classroom environment, then it must follow that there are clearly identifiable elements in that environment that contribute to the creation of what Fritz Redl, almost 50 years ago, called the therapeutic milieu.

The establishment of such a setting is a process that must be seen, when viewed historically, as differentiated from the management of the system. This chapter argues that the gap between establishment and management of classroom plans for mildly handicapped children must be closed. Regular classroom teachers are closest to the child, and their centrality to both planning and operationalizing programs is seminal to the achievement of successful outcomes. Three primary processes are critical in program development; each is treated separately here.

THE ROLE OF THE CLASSROOM TEACHER ON THE CHILD STUDY TEAM

The child study team has responsibility for collaborative decision making regarding program planning for children who are exceptional. For purposes of this discussion, we are interested in planning for those children whose needs are such that treatment in the regular classroom, with the use of supplementary aids and services, is a reasonable expectation.

School systems that are seriously committed to the education of mildly handicapped children in regular classrooms are characterized by smaller classroom size where handicapped children are included; by additional classroom personnel; by substantial commitments to the education of regular classroom teachers about children with special needs; and by increased supply budgets, including computer budgets that realistically reflect the use of newly emerging technologies in the instruction of children with special needs.

The decisions that make the difference between effective and ineffective regular classroom instruction for children with special needs are made by the child study team. In my experience, however, far too commonly the critical decisions that determine the degree to which the classroom serving the exceptional child is truly a therapeutic milieu are primarily driven by the contributions of those who knew the child only very briefly prior to the team meeting and who will have little or nothing to do with the child after the team reaches its decisions. In fact, one could, I suspect, quantifiably verify an inverse relationship between daily proximity to the child and degree of influence on the child study team. That is, the closer one is to the child under discussion, such as a parent or teacher, the less influence one is likely to have on the team's outcome. Conversely, those who know the child less well, but who carry a more highly valued status, such as administrators or clinicians, are likely to play a substantial, yet subtle, role in disenfranchising teachers and parents and thus dominating the decision-making process.

It is, therefore, arguable that the first, and perhaps most important, step in planning effective instruction for the special-needs child in the regular classroom is the influential participation of the regular classroom teacher in the child study team meeting. It is here, for example, that both classroom teachers and parents, those most clearly indispensable partners in the education of children, ought to be establishing every detail of the special-needs child's classroom placement. This often involves a process that, for some, will seem out of character and, consequently, very difficult. For instance, regular classroom teachers must begin to—

1. refuse to accept statements by diagnosticians, about a given child, that they believe to be inaccurate;
2. demand a lay translation of clinical language that they do not understand. When teachers are not clear about the language used by specialists who have evaluated the child, they have been effectively disenfranchised from the system;
3. refuse to accept support system arrangements for the integration of a child with special needs when they are convinced that the arrangement will lead only to dumping, not mainstreaming.

It has been my experience that teachers can accomplish these three objectives without rancor, bitterness, or adversarialism. They can achieve them with the highest degree of civility and professionalism. Classroom teachers have not, historically, asked such questions or made such demands. The change will certainly be obvious to everyone present. It is worth the effort, however, because change at this point in the process is otherwise not likely to occur.

Finally, I regularly advise teachers that a very important way to influence child study team decisions in ways that will result in improved regular classroom conditions for main-streamed students is to assure that their position on the important instructional issues is reflected in the minutes of the meeting. If that does not occur, then they should file a minority report. By either of these actions, teachers convey their serious doubt that the program, as proposed, can be effectively delivered in the regular classroom setting. This has a dual effect: first, it normally aligns parents with the classroom teacher who is seeking greater support services; and, second, it protects the teacher in the event that parents challenge the school later, through the due process mechanism available to them, regarding the efficacy of their child's program.

PREPARING YOUR CLASSROOM FOR THE INCLUSION OF CHILDREN WITH SPECIAL NEEDS

It has always struck me as interesting that authors write as if most classrooms have not had children with special needs all along. Naturally, they have. Until the past decade, however, we have not made a systematic, longitudinal effort to determine how we might manipulate the classroom environment to maximize its potential to operate most effectively for children with mild special needs.

Within the classroom setting, three techniques seem to have been most effective in developing empathy for children with special needs. This empathy, when fully developed, truly sets the stage for effective integration.

1. Simulation Exercises. Activities that place nonhandi-capped students in situations that simulate the

handicapping conditions of students in your class have proven to be very effective on a broad basis. These are easily implemented and several suggestions are available from the Council for Exceptional Children (1920 Association Drive, Reston, VA 22091–1589).

2. Cooperative Learning. Children teaching children is increasingly recognized as a helpful way to foster communication, collaboration, and understanding among students. The proximity within which the students must work for all to be successful operates as a functional magnet, drawing them all closer together.

3. Discussion Following Neutral Stimuli. The use of group discussion, paired with a stimulus that does not pertain personally to any of your students, but to which many of your students can relate, is often a strong inducement to the creation of empathy in your classroom. For example, a commercially available videotape portraying children with learning disabilities, or a group reading of children's literature portraying a child with mild learning problems, will generate much discussion and promote substantial understanding.

Special suggestions for videotapes include:

The ABC's of Teaching Disabled Children
American Federation of Teachers
555 New Jersey Avenue
Washington, DC 20001

Learning Disabilities: First Hand
Professional Research, Inc.
930 Pitner Avenue
Evanston, IL 60202

41

Classrooms as Systems

In our analysis of group settings, the notion of the classroom as a system, in which balance must be maintained for the system to function efficiently, is very different from the traditional view of classroom management. In the traditional perspective, classroom management was viewed from a child-centered pathological position. That is, management problems in classrooms were viewed as directly attributable to the deviant behavior of particular children who were, in turn, seen as pathological. In the systemic position described here, *systems* are seen as pathological, with the negative outcomes of that pathology being displayed through individual members of the system. Of course, in schools several systems merge: family systems, community systems, and school systems are all functions of the life of each member of the classroom group. Teachers have little ability to influence those factors that are external to the classroom setting. They do, however, have enormous ability to influence what happens when all the systems converge in the setting of the school.

Maintaining Systemic Balance

Negotiating one's way through the human maze that comprises the typical classroom setting involves the development of a plan that meets both the immediate and the long-term needs of all members of the system. Identification, then, of the needs that appear to be most common to children will be the first step toward the development of an interactional pattern that will permit those needs to be met.

For the purpose of the discussion, I wish to suggest three primary elements that may be seen as essential to the establishment of balanced classroom environments that, in turn, maximize the opportunity for children with special needs to deploy cognitive resources most efficiently. The singular importance of these elements cannot be overstated.

1. Structure. By structure, I refer to the establishment of clear boundaries. In dealing with children, lines of demarcation are critically important. While this is an important undertaking with all children, I have found it to be essential in those children who might best be referred to as "emotionally fragile."

The issue of boundary establishment extends beyond teaching children what is not permitted in the classroom. The environmental balancing act called group management demands that children's need for structure be met by us through several points, only one of which is the articulation of what is *not* allowed. Additionally, it is important for children to know, for example, what *is* allowed. Further, children seem to do best with clear signals indicating the beginning of the class day, the end of the class day, and important transition points within the day. Children, in sum, should never be placed in a position where they find out where the boundaries are only by crossing them.

2. Predictability. Not to be confused with boring! I think it possible to be predictable without assuring a six-hour daily nap for your students. Predictability is an essential element in maintaining low levels of anxiety in your group members. In my experience, I have found that the relationship between anxiety levels and behavior is as stable as a law of physics; with young children, high anxiety levels guarantee the production of high levels of acting-out behavior.

Children will generally work more efficiently in groups when they are able to assure themselves that nothing is going to happen with which they will be unfamiliar. Unfamiliar things, particularly those unfamiliar events that appear, to the child, to be personally threatening to him or her will increase anxiety to intolerable levels. The classroom environment, now subjected to what might well be termed "anxiety overload" from as many sources as there are children in the room, soon collapses as its adaptational mechanisms collapse. The result is usually a very disconnected classroom. While it may be arguable that any classroom is constantly in a transitional state merely because 20 to 30 people carry their "emotional baggage" into that setting daily, nevertheless there are limits to what the system can tolerate. It would be appropriate, therefore, to consider the notion of a group anxiety level that is tolerable, and then to consider defining, classroom by classroom, the point at which a lack of predictability drives the anxiety level past the limits wherein behavior is considered acceptable. Once that limit has been passed, the classroom environment can no longer normally be considered to be conducive to the good mental health of children or teachers.

3. Consistency. Discussions of consistency seem always to become entwined with discussions of predictability. They are, nevertheless, quite different. If predictability refers generally to the expectation that a certain response will be evoked by a specified stimulus, then consistency refers to the expectation that the scenario, as described, will occur with maximal frequency upon presentation of the same stimulus. Children must know that x generates y. That is predictability. They must also know that it will virtually always happen just that way. *That* is consistency.

Commonly, teachers respond to this notion of perpetual consistency by arguing, correctly, that to be so consistent is not to be human. In fact, they point out, as fallible beings we bring, on our *best* days, often uneven temperaments to the classroom. How then, they ask, can I ask for such perfection in terms of consistency? The answer, of course, is self-evident. Since it is human nature to be, to some degree, inconsistent, then a certain margin of inconsistency is seen as the standard by which all consistency is measured. In other words, one need not be perfect to maintain the primacy of consistency; one need only not go beyond the margin of error that can be expected to serve as the norm. When one does, anxiety levels and consequent acting out will surely occur.

BEYOND SYSTEMIC BALANCE

The three elements just described cannot wait for implementation in classrooms. Beyond these, however, the effective management of children in groups in ways that allow them to learn most effectively is dependent on the development of a long-term model of interaction that facilitates authentic communication during troubled moments within the classroom setting. In my work with teachers, we have settled on a model that genuinely embodies the principles of authenticity in relationships. This model is premised on the position that significant "therapists" in schools are classroom teachers.

The Elements of Effective Communication with Children

1. Decoding. Decoding refers to the process of interpreting messages from children. It includes both the "surface" message (the literal translation of what the child said) and the "other" message (what the child really meant but could not bring him/herself to say). Adults generally respond only to the surface message, thereby never receiving the actual content the child wished to convey, but what was transmitted in the guise of the surface message.

The chance of erring in the interpretation of the "other" message may be high. The teachers with whom I work and I, too, have found that an error in decoding usually shows itself to exist shortly after beginning the second or third step in this process.

2. Responding Empathetically. An empathetic response is one in which the receiver of the message responds with a communication that transmits a message to the child that he or she is highly valued, that his or her predicament is understood by the listener, and that the listener is ready to help the child help him/herself.

3. Clarifying. Clarifying is the process of leading children through a discussion of what *really* happened to cause whatever predicament they find themselves in at the moment.

This is a particularly important exercise because it implies that children must confront themselves with the reality of their own role in the causal chain. Through the teacher's prompting, the child must re-create and "walk" him/herself and the teacher through the event. Many of our most emotionally fragile children have become very adept at "lying to themselves." Our job is either to confirm their righteousness or to enable them to confront the delusions they have created to meet their needs.

4. Problem Solving. In this, the final step in this conversational process, we help children speculate on how they might have handled things differently. We hope, as a result of this exercise, that our children will make better choices the next time they are confronted with similar circumstances.

FINAL THOUGHTS

Group management of children is a process that is simpler than most academics would like to have us believe. The issues treated here—respect, caring, helping, structure; talking with, not talking *to*—all can be accomplished successfully with children by teachers who have the personal qualities that permit and even encourage them to engage groups of children in sincere interaction. There are no graphs, no charts, no stickers, no candy, no coupons to cash in—although I readily acknowledge the value of all those extrinsic reinforcers in certain situations. Those situations, however, and their extrinsic responses are, I submit, transient. The interpersonal communication model, established in an atmosphere of structure, predictability, and consistency, will pay systematic rewards to last children a lifetime.

DISCUSSION QUESTIONS

1. The author argues for a new approach to the child study team for the regular classroom teacher. In raising the issues he would like teachers to raise in that forum, aren't teachers taking substantial risks in terms of challenging the traditional decision makers? What could be the potential cost of this? What could be the potential benefit? What are the ethical issues involved and how might they be resolved?

2. The notion that the primary therapists in schools are really not those people whose roles are defined as therapist (counselors, social workers, etc.) but are classroom teachers, is clearly different from our traditional view. What constitutes school-based therapy and who can best carry it out?

3. If the author is correct in his assessment of the demise of the perceptual deficit hypothesis, why is it that we see some students improve when they are treated, individually or in small groups, with perceptual motor training? Could there be an explanation that is unrelated to the perceptual motor training itself, but is still a plausible rationale?

Chapter 3

ASSESSING STUDENTS WITH SPECIAL NEEDS: CURRENT AND EMERGING PERSPECTIVES

by Libby G. Cohen

Libby Cohen stresses that assessment is critical in the planning and delivery of instruction. Although the assessment of students with special needs is regulated by federal and state laws, the classification of students into categories, according to handicapping condition, has received much criticism. Emerging trends point toward a closer link between assessment and instruction through the use of curriculum-based assessment.

Why is assessment important? Assessment plays a crucial role in the planning and delivery of instruction. The curriculum that is taught, the instructional approaches that are used, the instructional goals that are developed, and the instructional materials that are used are all affected by the assessment process. The results of assessment determine which students are eligible to receive special services, the development and planning of individual goals, the evaluation of these goals, and when students exit education.

This chapter provides an overview of several different types of assessment activities that are used in making educational decisions about students with special needs. It discusses the major components of federal legislation regarding the classification and assessment of these students. It also explains curriculum-based assessment, an emerging trend in the evaluation of students with special needs.

DEFINITION OF ASSESSMENT

According to Salvia and Ysseldyke (14), assessment is "the process of collecting data for the purpose of (1) specifying and verifying problems and (2) making decisions about students" (p. 5). Five types of decisions can be made: (1) screening and identification, (2) classification and placement, (3) instructional planning, (4) determining pupil progress, and (5) program evaluation.

THE EDUCATION FOR ALL HANDICAPPED CHILDREN ACT

The assessment and classification of children is highly regulated in the United States. The Education for All Handicapped Children Act, more commonly referred to as P.L. 94–142, passed by Congress in 1975, mandates activities that schools must undertake in order to serve children with handicaps.

In the school year 1987–88, there were 3,485,088 children in the United States who were classified as handicapped (21). According to P.L. 94–142, the following categories are defined as handicapped: deaf, deaf-blind, hard of hearing, mentally retarded, multihandicapped, orthopedically impaired, seriously emotionally disturbed, specific learning disability, speech impaired, and visually handicapped. The largest categories are learning disabled, speech impaired, mentally retarded, and emotionally disturbed (21).

Although the classification of students into categories and their placement into special education have been criticized, almost all state special education laws parallel the federal law. An emerging trend is that some states, while reporting students on a categorical basis to the federal government, do not categorize students for placement into special education.

P.L. 94–142 contains major provisions regarding the testing and assessment of students who may have special needs:

1. Tests and evaluation materials must not be racially or culturally discriminatory.
2. Before the child can be placed in a special education program, a complete individual evaluation of the child's educational needs must be undertaken.
3. Tests and evaluation materials must be administered in the child's native language, unless it is not feasible to do so.
4. Tests and evaluation materials must be administered by trained personnel.
5. Tests and other evaluation materials must be validated for the purposes for which they are used.
6. Tests and other evaluation materials must assess specific areas of educational need, not just those that provide a single estimate of intellectual functioning.
7. Tests and evaluation materials are administered to best ensure that when a test is administered to a child who is impaired, the test results will accurately reflect the child's aptitude or achievement level rather than the child's impaired sensory, manual, or speaking skills (except where those skills are the factors that the test purports to measure).
8. More than one instrument must be used.
9. A multidisciplinary team must evaluate the child.
10. The child must be evaluated in all areas of the suspected disability including, where appropriate, health, vision, hearing, social and emotional status, general intelligence, academic performance, communicative status, and motor abilities.
11. The child must be reevaluated every three years unless the parents or teachers request an evaluation sooner. (Adapted from P.L. 94–142, *Federal Register,* pp. 42496–97)

SHOULD STUDENTS WITH HANDICAPS BE CLASSIFIED?

Within the past few years, the classification of students by handicapping condition has received a great deal of criticism. In a review of the literature on assessing students who are handicapped, Ysseldyke (23) wrote that although federal law and most state laws mandate the classification of students, there is no psychometric approach that reliably differentiates students into categories. In addition, the classification and placement of students into categorical groups is not a logical, useful, or acceptable practice.

Classification of students can also produce harmful side effects (10, 13). Just the act of labeling a child can be deleterious. When children are labeled they may feel stigmatized. Labels may also give rise to the self-fulfilling prophecy in which teachers and parents may raise or lower their expectations of the student depending on the label. And labels may unfairly discriminate among certain racial and ethnic groups.

Research conducted at the University of Minnesota initially examined the assessment process for students who were labeled learning disabled (24); the results raised strong criticisms of current special education assessment practices. Among their conclusions, the researchers found that

> the special education decision-making process is one in which a student is referred, often for vague and subjective reasons; automatically tested, often with technically inadequate devices; usually placed by a team meeting; and is the object of decisions made less on data than on subjective teacher or student variables and on inconsistent and indefensible criteria. (24, p. 87)

STANDARDIZED TESTS

Standardized tests are typically used to assist in making assessment decisions. These tests are also known as norm-referenced tests because the scores are based on the average performance of a norm group. Test publishers develop the test questions and administer the test to a large group of students called the standardization sample or the norm group, which has been carefully selected to represent certain demographic characteristics such as geographic location, race, ethnic group, gender, grade in school, and age. Because standardized tests are developed to facilitate the making of comparisons between students, they are used in special education to make screening, placement, diagnostic, and classification decisions about students.

Many criticisms of norm-referenced standardized tests have been raised within recent years. For example, they may be biased toward certain cultural groups, minorities, and those to whom English is a second language (7, 19, 22). The results of standardized tests may not adequately measure prior experiences or individual learning styles (12). Commercially published norm-referenced tests in academic areas may not adequately measure the contemporary approaches to the teaching of reading, mathematics, science, and other academic areas. According to Shriner and Salvia, "Special educators should no longer accept the results of standardized achievement tests unless they have been demonstrated to match a student's curricula" (16, p. 248).

CRITERION-REFERENCED TESTS

Criterion-referenced tests compare a student's performance with a specified criterion, not with the performance of other students. For example, when assessing a student's reading skills, a criterion-referenced test provides information on how well the student performs in relation to specified curriculum objectives or goals.

Despite the attractiveness of criterion-referenced tests, they too have been criticized for several reasons. Smith (17) believes that they do not tell us how a student organizes information or processes it. Because the results of criterion-referenced testing provide only information on which curriculum objectives were met and which ones were not met, the teacher is left wondering about the effectiveness of the instruction or intervention that was provided. In addition, many commercially published criterion-referenced tests share a similar criticism of standardized tests in that many items may not correspond to the curriculum.

CURRICULUM-BASED ASSESSMENT

An emerging trend, curriculum-based assessment directly links what has been taught with the assessment process. Curriculum-based assessment is "the practice of obtaining direct and frequent measurement of student performance on a series of sequentially arranged educational objectives derived from the curriculum used in the classroom" (1, p. 234). Marston and Magnusson (11) stated that its primary purpose is to assist the instructional process.

Curriculum-based assessment puts teachers in a central role in the assessment process (1). As Tucker pointed out:

Curriculum-based assessment (CBA) is the ultimate in "teaching the test," because the materials used to assess progress are *always* drawn directly from the course of study. Thus, in CBA reading level and reading ability are assessed by having the student read material from the school's own curriculum (20, p. 200).

Curriculum-based assessment is attractive because teachers can develop, administer, and score the test instruments. Because the teacher knows the curriculum and because the curriculum-based assessment instrument has been developed by the teacher, the test provides a direct link to instruction. The teacher can thus use the results of the testing to determine the benefits of instruction, to modify instruction, and to develop new instructional goals. Some curriculum-based instruments can be used to make placement, grouping, and referral decisions. For further information, readers may want to examine books and journal articles cited in the References by Tucker (20), Gickling and Thompson (9), Deno (3), Germann and Tindal (8), Shinn (15), and Deno and Fuchs (4).

The use of curriculum-based assessment can be compared with variations on a theme (2). It is not just one approach to testing and instruction. Because curriculum-based assessment is an attractive alternative and adjunct to norm-referenced standardized testing, teachers may want to develop their own instruments. As previously mentioned, there is not just one approach to this type of assessment. First, a general approach to developing a curriculum-based assessment instrument will be discussed. Then, a specific approach, curriculum-based measurement, will be described.

A general approach to constructing a curriculum-based assessment instrument consists of five steps (see Figure 1):

1. Identify the purpose of the curriculum-based assessment instrument. This may be to measure achievement, determine instructional needs, screen students, or diagnose or place students.
2. Develop test specifications or curriculum objectives. The teacher should develop test specifications that specify the content, the cognitive operations that the student will be asked to perform, the response types, and the level of proficiency that the student will demonstrate. As an alternative, teachers can specify the curriculum objectives that will be tested.
3. Construct the test items; review and, if necessary, revise the test.
4. Administer the test. During the testing, the classroom should be quiet, free of distractions, well lighted, and comfortable.
5. Develop norms or graph performance. If the test is to be used for classification and placement decisions, it

must be normed. Teachers should consult an introductory statistics book for norming procedures. If instructional progress is monitored, student performance can be graphed.

Figure 1
Steps in Constructing a
Curriculum-Based Assessment Instrument

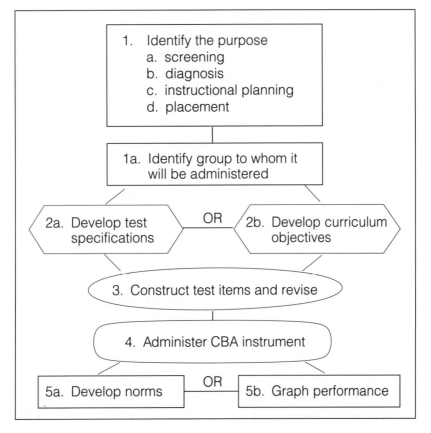

From Cohen, L. G. "Development of a Curriculum-Based Assessment Instrument." In *A Practical Guide to Curriculum-Based Assessment for Special Educators,* edited by L. G. Cohen and J. Spruill, 1990. Courtesy of Charles C. Thomas, Publisher, Springfield, Illinois.

CURRICULUM-BASED MEASUREMENT

Curriculum-based measurement is a specific approach to curriculum-based assessment that has received wide attention (3, 4). This approach is characterized by direct, frequent, and repeated measures across various curriculum areas. Abundant research has supported the reliability and validity of measures of these instruments in reading, spelling, written expression, and mathematics (3, 5, 15).

Procedures on how to develop, administer, and score curriculum-based measurement instruments have been developed for these four areas. With this approach, reading fluency (speed and accuracy of reading) is measured. To develop a curriculum-based measurement instrument in reading, the teacher prepares two copies of a reading passage (which the teacher randomly selects from the student's own reading book), one for the teacher and one for the student. The teacher says to the child:

> When I say "start," begin reading aloud at the top of this page. Read across the page (demonstrate by pointing). Try to read each word. If you come to a word you don't know, I'll tell it to you. Be sure to do your best reading. Are there any questions? (15, p. 239).

While the student reads, the teacher follows along in the teacher's copy of the reading material, indicating any words that the student reads incorrectly or with which the student has difficulty. After one minute, the student is asked to stop reading. The total number of words read correctly is the student's score. Words that have been mispronounced, substituted, or omitted are considered errors and are not counted. It is recommended that the teacher measure the student's reading ability several times a week, using this procedure (15).

Written expression is measured by a story starter that the teacher has developed. The teacher directs the student as follows:

I want you to write a story. I am going to read a sentence to you first, and then I want you to write a short story about what happens. You will have one minute to think about the story you will write and then have three minutes to write it. Do your best work. If you don't know how to spell a word, you should guess. Are there any questions? (15, p. 240)

The student is then told to think about the story starter for one minute and then to begin writing. The student is instructed to write for three minutes. There are four ways to score the writing sample: (1) count the total words written, (2) count the words spelled correctly, (3) count the total number of letters written, and (4) count correct word sequences (a correct word sequence is at least two words that are joined that are spelled correctly and that are grammatically correct) (15).

In spelling, the teacher can choose a list of words from a spelling list or from the student's reading materials. The words are dictated, individually or to a group of students, for a period of two minutes. The teacher is instructed to pause for 10 seconds between words for students in grades 1 to 3 (the total number of words dictated will be approximately 12–13); to pause for 7 seconds for students above grade 3 (the total number of words dictated will be approximately 17–18). The student's score is the total number of words spelled correctly or the number of correct letter sequences (15).

To construct a curriculum-based measurement test in mathematics, the teacher selects problems from curriculum-related materials. The test can be a single skill probe or a multiple skill probe. The student is instructed to begin work and not to skip around, and to stop working after two minutes. The student's score is the total number of correctly written (and answered) digits (15).

With the curriculum-based measurement approach, the teacher administers the tests two to three times a week and graphs the student's performance. By frequently measuring performance, instruction can be modified to meet the instructional needs of the student. But this approach has been criticized because it stresses the isolation of skills rather than emphasizing the learning process. And the use of graphs, which represent learning in a linear fashion, is an oversimplification of the learning process and the assessment of this learning. However, it may be motivating to the learner to be able to visualize progress in the form of a graph.

CAUTIONS AND CONCERNS

Curriculum-based assessment is an alternative to traditional methods of testing. But Taylor, Willits, and Richards (18), while recommending its use, raised important concerns about this method. They believe that curriculum-based assessment (CBA) is appropriate—

If the curriculum on which CBA is based is valid

If the curriculum on which the CBA is based represents the needs of the special education student

If the CBA instrument can be developed to yield reliable and valid results

If limitations are acknowledged or additional research is conducted regarding the curricular areas for which CBA is appropriate

If limitations are acknowledged regarding the use of CBA as a comprehensive assessment approach

If careful attention is given to properly training users of CBA. (18, p. 20)

While curriculum-based assessment is not without its problems, this approach to measuring student learning is appealing. It is the practice of good instructional techniques. It directly links assessment to what has been taught and to planning and modifying what should be taught. Instruments can be developed for different areas of the curriculum. Most importantly, it is very useful in planning and modifying instruction for students with special needs.

OTHER ASSESSMENT APPROACHES

In addition to the use of norm-referenced standardized tests, criterion-referenced tests, and curriculum-based assessment, there are many other ways to collect information about student performance. These include other types of teacher-made tests, unpublished tests, student interviews, classroom observations, rating scales, clinical judgment, and diagnostic teaching.

When should these different approaches be used? The answer is, it all depends on the purpose of the assessment activity. When classification, identification, and placement decisions must be made, a norm-referenced standardized test should be used. For planning instruction, determining pupil progress, and evaluating the program a variety of instruments can be used. This chapter has discussed three of these activities: standardized testing, criterion-referenced testing, and curriculum-based assessment.

Among the many useful books that discuss assessment activities, the following are recommended:

Board of Education for the City of Etobicoke. *Making the Grade.* Scarborough, Canada: Prentice-Hall of Canada, 1987.

Evans, S. S.; Evans, W. H.; and Mercer, C. D. *Assessment for Instruction.* Boston, Mass.: Allyn and Bacon, 1986.

Goodman, K. S.; Goodman, Y. M.; and Hood, W. J. *The Whole Language Evaluation Book.* Portsmouth, N.H.: Heineman, 1989.

Guerin, G. R., and Maier, A. S. *Informal Assessment in Education.* Palo Alto, Calif.: Mayfield, 1983.

PREFERRED PRACTICES

Based on emerging trends, teachers are encouraged to use the following preferred practices relating to assessment:

1. Maintain confidentiality of information about students.

2. When referring students, adhere to the legal requirements found in P.L. 94–142, state laws, and local policies, regarding evaluation of students.
3. Refer students for special education evaluations only after modifying and adapting instructional, environmental, and ecological conditions.
4. Frequently assess and monitor the performance of ALL your students. Directly link instruction with assessment.
5. After modifying or adapting instruction, assess in order to determine whether the modifications have benefited the student.
6. Provide frequent feedback of progress to the student and to the parents.
7. Be aware of alternatives to standardized testing.
8. Use a variety of assessment approaches including curriculum-based assessment, standardized testing, interviews, and observations.

DISCUSSION QUESTIONS

1. Reflect on your school's current policies for classifying and identifying students with special needs. What recommendations would you make to improve the policies and the process?
2. In what ways is the classification of students by handicapping condition harmful? Beneficial?
3. Compare the curriculum and textbooks that your students use with the standardized tests that are administered to them. What are the differences and the similarities?
4. How could curriculum-based assessment be useful to you?

ACKNOWLEDGMENT

Material from *Curriculum-Based Measurement—Assessing Special Children*, edited by M. R. Shinn, pp. 239–42, is reprinted and/or adapted with permission of the publisher. Copyright © 1989 by Guilford Press.

REFERENCES

1. Blankenship, C. S. "Using Curriculum-Based Assessment Data to Make Instructional Decisions." *Exceptional Children* 52, no. 3 (November 1985): 232–38.
2. Cohen, L. G., and Spence, S. "Methods of Implementation." In *A Practical Guide to Curriculum-Based Assessment for Special Educators,* edited by L. Cohen and J. Spruill. Springfield, Ill.: Charles Thomas. 1990.
3. Deno, S. "Curriculum-Based Assessment: The Emerging Alternative." *Exceptional Children* 52, no. 3 (November 1985): 219–32.
4. Deno, S. L., and Fuchs, L. S. "Developing Curriculum-Based Measurement Systems for Data-Based Special Education Problem Solving." *Focus on Exceptional Children* 19 (April 1987): 1–15.
5. Deno, S. L.; Marston, D.; and Mirkin, P. "Valid Measurement Procedures for Continuous Evaluation of Written Expression." *Exceptional Children* 48, no. 4 (November 1982): 368–71.
6. *Federal Register* (August 23, 1977): 42474–42518.
7. Galagan, J. E. "Psychoeducational Testing: Turn Out the Lights, the Party's Over." *Exceptional Children* 52, no. 3 (November 1985): 288–99.
8. Germann, G., and Tindal, D. "An Application of Curriculum-Based Assessment: The Use of Direct and Repeated Measurement." *Exceptional Children* 52, no. 3 (November 1985): 244–65.
9. Gickling, E. E., and Thompson, V. P. "A Personal View of Curriculum-Based Assessment." *Exceptional Children* 52, no. 3 (November 1985): 205–18.
10. Hobbs, N. *The Futures of Children.* San Francisco: Jossey-Bass, 1975.
11. Marston, D., and Magnusson, D. "Implementing Curriculum-Based Assessment in Special and Regular Educational Settings." *Exceptional Children* 52, no. 3 (November 1985): 266–72.
12. Meyers, J.; Pfeffer, J.; and Erlbaum, V. "Process Assessment: A Model for Broadening Assessment." *Journal of Special Education* 18, no. 2 (Summer 1985): 1–84.
13. Reynolds, M. C., and Birch, J. W. *Adaptive Mainstreaming.* New York: Longman, 1988.

14. Salvia, J., and Ysseldyke, J. E. *Assessment in Special and Remedial Education.* 4th ed. Boston: Houghton Mifflin, 1988.
15. Shinn, M. R., ed. *Curriculum-Based Measurement—Assessing Special Children.* New York: Guilford Press, 1989.
16. Shriner, J., and Salvia, J. "Chronic Noncorrespondence Between Elementary Math Curricula and Arithmetic Tests." *Exceptional Children* 55, no. 3 (November 1988): 240–48.
17. Smith, C. R. "Assessment Alternatives: Non-Standardized Procedures." *School Psychology Review* 1, no. 9 (Winter 1980): 46–56.
18. Taylor, R. L.; Willits, P. P.; and Richards, S. B. "Curriculum-Based Assessment: Considerations and Concerns." *Diagnostique* 14 (Fall 1988): 14–21.
19. Tindal, G., and Marston, D. *Approaches to Assessment: Psychoeducational Perspectives on Learning Disabilities.* San Diego: Academic Press, 1986.
20. Tucker, J. A. "Curriculum-Based Assessment: An Introduction." *Exceptional Children* 52, no. 3 (November 1985): 199–204.
21. U.S. Department of Education. *To Assure the Free Appropriate Public Education of All Handicapped Children, Ninth Annual Report to Congress.* Washington, D.C.: U.S. Department of Education, 1989.
22. Webster, R.; McInnis, E.; and Carver, L. "Curriculum Biasing Effects in Standardized and Criterion-Referenced Reading Achievement Tests." *Psychology in the Schools* 23, no. 2 (April 1986): 205–13.
23. Ysseldyke, J. "Classification of Handicapped Students." In *Handbook of Special Education: Research and Practice,* Vol. 1, edited by M. C. Wang, M. Reynolds, and H. Walberg, 253–71. Oxford: Pergamon, 1987.
24. Ysseldyke, J. E.; Thurlow, M.; Graden, J.; Wesson, C.; Algozzine, B.; and Deno, S. "Generalizations from Five Years of Research on Assessment and Decision-Making." *Exceptional Education Quarterly* 14, no. 1 (Spring 1983): 75-92.

Chapter 4

STUDENTS WITH MILD HANDICAPS IN SECONDARY CLASSROOMS

by Jo Anna Spruill

Building on the previous chapters, Jo Anna Spruill examines the mainstream academic experiences of adolescents with mild learning handicaps. She presents common characteristics of secondary students with mild handicaps and compares these to the demands of mainstream academic classes. She also explores general accommodations that can be made in classrooms through collaboration among special education and regular education teachers. In addition, she describes specific instructional strategies that have proven effective with special education and other low-achieving students. Finally, she recommends that students with learning difficulties be given the opportunity to acquire and practice basic skills and learning strategies within the context of regular classroom content.

By far the commonest educational placements for secondary level students with learning handicaps are in mainstream classes with typical peers. Frequently, mildly learning handicapped students can be distinguished from nonhandicapped students on the basis of deficits believed to interfere with academic functioning, including language ability, academic achievement, functioning related to memory, attention, and perception, and the appropriateness of their social behavior (12). At times, however, the variance between these populations is not adequately explained. Although mildly handicapped students

63

derive many benefits from mainstream placements, they often need special assistance from regular teachers, support teachers, and their peers. When these support structures are in place, mildly handicapped students thrive, but when the students are ill prepared and inadequately supported in their classes, they may assume passive or defensive postures throughout their mainstream experiences. This chapter describes strategies that the secondary teacher can use when teaching students who are mildly learning handicapped.

There are several reasons why students with disabilities are included in mainstream classes. At this point in history when society is experiencing a technological revolution, jobs require technical, problem-solving, and literacy skills as never before. Most individuals will need postsecondary job training or education in order to develop the skills needed to earn an adequate living. Preparation at the secondary level that takes place in integrated environments is the most realistic and effective preparation for future activities in integrated settings, such as college, technical school, and competitive employment.

The transition from secondary schools to postsecondary education is a particularly difficult one for students with mild learning handicaps, and the outcomes have not been good. Few of these students continue their education beyond high school, and of those who do (mainly students at technical or trade schools), very few complete training (20). Students who are interested in postsecondary education should have at least fifth and sixth grade functional skills in reading and mathematics by the ninth grade (14), average or better than average verbal intellectual ability, and the skills and opportunities to take a modified schedule of college preparatory courses. In general, learning handicapped students have not fared well in academic mainstream courses. A study of report cards of ninth grade learning-disabled students revealed that 74 percent of the students earned grades of D or less in social studies, 69 percent had D or less in science, and 63 percent D or less in health. It was discouraging to learn that the overall grade average for ninth grade learning-disabled (LD) students was .99 on a four-point scale (20).

Some reasons for the difficulties low-achieving students have in academic courses may be found in the frequent mismatch of learner characteristics with the information-processing conditions found in many classrooms. Learning handicapped students often face the challenge of learning new information without the knowledge base that facilitates new learning. They must monitor a wide band of information sources that are presented in various forms and on various levels of intensity. They are expected to come to class prepared with equipment and ready to discern, among the plentiful and rapidly changing stimuli, hints and clues that will guide them in preparing for examinations and other assignments. Furthermore, students need well-developed social comprehension and communication skills to gain assistance, to present themselves in an appealing manner to teachers, and to be socially acceptable to their peers. Learning handicapped students frequently number these abilities among their areas of weaknesses.

CHARACTERISTICS OF CLASSROOMS

The characteristics of typical classrooms may contribute to the difficulties that students with mild handicaps have in secondary schools. Instruction often consists of teacher-directed, whole-class, individualistic and competitive activities (20). Frequently, several events are occurring simultaneously. Many classrooms are dominated by student-initiated social interactions (17). Some students come to school with an agenda formed primarily by their personal issues. The classroom becomes an additional arena for playing out reactions to family or developmental concerns. In a recent study of classroom interactions (17), students demonstrated numerous strategies for taking the focus off academic tasks, for getting assignments that present a low level of risk, and for arranging ample opportunities to socialize.

In general, we may portray classrooms as multidimensional, unpredictable, and frequently torn by conflicting personal agendas. There is little opportunity for students to interrupt the mass processing system that makes up a classroom (5). Students with certain abilities are more successful than others in negotiating the classroom terrain. Those who can exercise perceptual selectivity, who can process information rapidly, and who have a good sense of timing, the patience to attend to unstimulating sources of information, and the motivation to resist social interactions are most likely to meet with success in mainstream classrooms (5, 17). Mildly learning handicapped students who take mainstream courses commonly lack these characteristics.

CHARACTERISTICS OF STUDENTS WITH MILD LEARNING HANDICAPS

Some recent studies of learning handicapped secondary students help to explain why they have such a difficult time in mainstream classrooms. An analysis of the National High School and Beyond Study (9) found that 2.7 percent of the sample self-identified as mildly handicapped. These students reported a significantly higher incidence of problems with self-image, locus of control, and contacts with the law. At the classroom level, the typical learning handicapped student is believed to be "a passive learner who comes to class ill-equipped for the lesson, goofs off during about 40 percent of class time, follows teachers' procedural directions, avoids giving information, and seldom volunteers a comment or asks a question" (19, p. 10).

Academic Behaviors

In regard to academic pursuits, a picture emerges of mildly handicapped secondary students as poor at organizing

66

materials, taking notes, identifying main ideas of written and spoken information, following directions, and completing and turning in assignments (2, 19). As writers (8), these students exhibit difficulty in planning and generating text. While they produce very brief essays and frequently omit story endings and conclusions to arguments, they *do* include a fair amount of irrelevant and unneeded material. Analyses of the written products of learning handicapped students suggest a major deficit in attending to the point of view and needs of the reader (8). Their deficits in written expression on the level of mechanics, (e.g., letter and word formation, spacing, fluency), their below-average listening skills, and their slow rate of processing easily account for weaknesses in note-taking.

The mismatch between classroom characteristics and demands and the characteristics of learning handicapped students is quite clear. Secondary teachers rate attendance, completing assignments, and showing an interest in learning as most important for success in their courses, while LD students display higher rates of absenteeism, fewer completed assignments, and poor attention to information sources (20). Classrooms are characterized by simultaneous occurrences and a variety of information sources requiring selectivity in information processing. These students, on the other hand, tend to be passive learners, poor organizers, and inadept note-takers. In addition, LD students have trouble recognizing important information and expressing information in written form. It appears that there is ample reason for concern about the quality of the mainstream experience for secondary students with mild handicaps.

GENERAL ACCOMMODATIONS FOR STUDENTS

If students are to reverse their trend to plateau academically at an early secondary level (sixth to eighth grade), the goals of mainstream placements must go beyond socialization to target basic skill development and improvement in learning strategies. There are many accommodations that can be made at the secondary level to improve the academic learning outcomes of students with mild handicaps in mainstream classes. These accommodations fit into several categories: collaborative activities, administrative arrangements, and support structures. This section describes steps secondary educators can take to improve the opportunities students have to prepare themselves for postsecondary education, vocational training, and employment.

Collaboration

Collaboration is a key element in instructional delivery to students in mainstream classes. Counselors and special educators join in communicating to classroom teachers the students' behavioral and learning characteristics and the academic goals and recommendations contained in the students' Individualized Education Plans (IEPs). Mainstream teachers should know the important details of the students' academic strengths and weaknesses, interests, and preferred methods of expression. Teachers also must know how to assist students to prepare for their postsecondary goals.

Regular and special education teachers may collaborate in using curriculum-based assessment (CBA) to determine appropriate mainstream placements and to plan the support students will need. CBA instruments may consist of reading passages randomly chosen from textbooks used in targeted mainstream courses. The results can be used to determine the suitability of a text for specific students and to aid staff in preparing and supporting students for mainstream classes. To assess fluency and skill in written expression, prospective mainstreamed students will listen to a lecture and take notes, or they may simply write for three minutes after reading a story starter and thinking for one minute. The closer the assessment task to how the skill will be used in mainstream classes, the more valid the assessment results. After students' performances have been compared to those obtained from assessment of a group of typical students, a support plan is devised for students as needed.

Administrative Arrangements

Administrative arrangements refer to the components of instructional delivery that require planning and approval from school administrators, such as class configuration, team teaching assignments, and modifications to curriculum content and evaluative procedures. Some school systems have had success with team teaching between special and regular teachers for classes of 15 to 25 students with average to low-average academic skills. Team teaching appears to increase student time on task, provide opportunities for individualizing instruction, and increase students' chances of receiving feedback and additional instruction without interrupting the progress of the curriculum. The team teaching component has also been successful between two regular education teachers with the same number of students.

At times it is important to develop flexible approaches for assignment of grades and credits. Sometimes tests are modified to meet the needs of individual students by restating questions, reducing the number of choices in multiple-choice questions, and changing the location or form of test presentation. It may be necessary, at times, to modify the course requirements for credit to suit the needs of individual students and the goals and objectives stated on their IEPs. As long as administrators feel comfortable that mildly handicapped students are profiting from their mainstream experiences and that the modifications make these experiences possible, they are usually agreeable to creative arrangements.

Support Structures

Mainstream teachers often rely upon special education teachers to support the special needs of students who are taking their courses. The support may take several forms, including learning strategies instruction, tutoring, and preparation of advance organizers and other specialized materials. A learning strategies curriculum, such as that developed at the University of Kansas (1), teaches students to write well-structured paragraphs and edit them, to apply a systematic approach to textbook study and problem solving, and to prepare for tests. Often, learning strategies instruction is undertaken in a resource room setting and then applied to assignments in mainstream courses. The collaborating teachers evaluate students' performances and make adjustments as needed.

Another form of support is tutorial assistance to aid students in completing assignments, preparing for tests, and comprehending difficult concepts. Tutorial assistance is typically supplied by special education teachers or trained peer tutors. The special education department may also supply specialized teaching materials, such as audiotapes of texts and other books, advance organizers, study guides, and modified teaching materials.

The success of mainstream placements often depends upon the strength of the collaboration between regular education and special education, the creativity and appropriateness of administrative arrangements, and the effectiveness of support structures developed for mildly learning handicapped students.

INSTRUCTIONAL STRATEGIES

In the classroom, it is the teacher's job to promote student behaviors that foster academic achievement. New learning that builds on past learning is facilitated through repetition, elaboration, and reorganization of information (7, p. 531). Teachers can also aid achievement by assigning tasks that motivate involvement, hold the students' attention, and require active processing of information. While some student characteristics, such as short-term memory, spatial concept ability, and the ability to engage in thinking that goes beyond the immediate context, may be individual givens, other student characteristics can be altered. These characteristics include the effectiveness of their learning strategies, their ability to use support structures, and the extent of their subject-related knowledge (7). Teachers can help students become aware of and manage more successfully their study skills, support opportunities, and personal resources. Teachers can also manipulate the learning environment. A classroom environment that promotes achievement is one that is warm and encouraging, promotes friendships and support, has little noise and interruptions, provides easy access to the teacher and materials, and focuses primarily on academic tasks (7).

Effective Instructional Techniques

According to Brophy (cited in Christenson, Ysseldyke, and Thurlow [4]), instructional effectiveness requires that teachers master many teaching techniques and acquire the knowledge and skills to select and use specific techniques at appropriate times. The following instructional factors are among those identified through research as critical to learning by students with mild handicaps:

- Ambitious, but reasonable, stated goals;
- Clarity in identifying for students the performance expectations;
- High rate of opportunities for correct responses by students;
- High rate of and efficient use of time-on-task;
- Continuous teacher monitoring of progress and feedback to students;
- Seatwork that is explained, justified, and monitored by the classroom teacher;
- Frequent and appropriate evaluation;
- Explicit feedback on accuracy of student responses and, if negative, specific steps for correcting their performance;
- Use of effective motivational techniques, such as challenges and reinforcement;

71

- Lessons plans that follow the model for direct instruction;
- Use of advance organizers (study guides, outlines) and summaries (oral or written);
- Instruction in the use of memory aides (imagery, elaboration, mnemonics);
- Student explanations of and strategies for problem solving (4).

Although this list is not exhaustive, these strategies have been repeatedly identified as sound instructional practices.

TEACHING LESSONS

There are many accommodations in planning lessons that teachers can make to benefit low-achieving students in their classrooms. If students are to make significant gains in basic skills, mainstream teachers must do more than present subject matter; they must also provide students an opportunity to relearn and to practice basic skills and applications related to reading, writing, and numerical calculation. A direct instruction lesson structure is effective in transmitting information to students and in building specific academic skills. Teachers may provide students with supplemental opportunities to process information through rehearsal, reorganization, and elaboration activities. At the practice stage, cooperative learning groups provide an opportunity for low-achieving students to receive support and reteaching from their peers. Finally, compensatory accommodations in presenting information, doing evaluations, and assigning grades make mainstream classrooms viable alternatives for students with mild learning handicaps.

Lesson Structure

The direct instruction lesson structure is consistently correlated with academic achievement for low-achieving students (5, 13) and is appropriate for use in introducing curricular topics and teaching specific skills. The direct instruction lesson format has the following sequence:

1. Gain the learner's attention. Verbal prompting may include remarks like "Look here." "Listen." "Let's begin." A satisfactory criterion for maintaining student involvement in teacher-directed activities is 90 percent task engagement.
2. Review relevant past learning. Establish a link between new information and what students already know.
3. Communicate the goal of the lesson. Low-achieving students learn best when teachers briefly state what is being learned, why it is important, and how it relates to other learning.
4. Model the skill to be learned. Steps should proceed in small increments, with explicit instructions and exaggeration to highlight critical features.
5. Prompt for correct response. Effective teaching includes guided practice with prompts and feedback to elicit correct responses.
6. Check for skill mastery. Students perform the behavior under close supervision with no prompting.
7. Close the lesson. Review the skill and discuss what will be covered in the next lesson (6).

Lessons based on this sequence are particularly effective for presenting factual information and vocabulary and for teaching problem-solving strategies.

Opportunities for Practice

Many students with learning difficulties need extra opportunities for rehearsal, reorganization, and the elaboration of concepts and information in order to commit them to long-term memory. One means of rehearsing is through whole-class drill activities, teacher- or student-led small group activities, or taped lessons for a selected group of students. Students also learn through exercises that involve reorganization of essential ideas and information. These exercises may take many forms: reteaching by peers, restatement of notes onto study guides, or paraphrasing and distilling information to its critical content. Another approach to committing information to long-term memory is through elaboration of ideas during application activities, such as participating in group projects, preparing for and writing essays, debating, and making in-class presentations.

Grouping for cooperative learning is a technique that has received attention as an effective means of meeting general classroom goals while supporting low-achieving students in the mainstream environment. Through this approach students are assigned to heterogeneous groups, are instructed in the goals and procedures for cooperatively completing assigned tasks, and share equally in the evaluation and grading process. These groups allow advanced students to benefit from assuming the role of facilitator or teacher. Low-achieving students may practice or may be retaught content, as well as contribute to activities at their own ability level. Readers are directed to the literature on cooperative learning, especially the work of David and Roger Johnson (10) of the University of Minnesota and Robert E. Slavin (15).

Compensatory Accommodations

There is a place, as well, for compensatory accommodations for students with handicaps in integrated programs. Many approaches have been developed, only a few of which are described here. Students frequently need help in gaining access to the curriculum content as it is presented in class and in textbooks. Learning handicapped students may wish to tape lectures or obtain copies of lecture notes from nonhandicapped classmates. They may use volunteers to read the textbooks to them, or they may benefit from listening to the texts on audiotapes. In addition, these students can be paired with a peer tutor or may join a study group for test preparation. Personal computers are also playing a central role in supporting low-achieving students. They are used for motivating performance, supplying additional practice, developing interactive problem-solving skills, and word processing. Computers assist students in composition through editing and rewriting capabilities and through programs that check spelling, grammar, and style.

Students with learning disabilities may need accommodations that go beyond altering the format of information presentation and technical supports. At times they will require accommodations to curriculum requirements, grading practices, and testing procedures. For some students it may be unrealistic to expect them to meet the full range of curricular goals. For these students, the educational planning team will identify from course objectives those that are appropriate for individuals. The planning team may also establish appropriate modified testing procedures and grading guidelines for individual students. Regular and special educators collaborate to implement special policies by adapting assignments and testing formats that focus the student's activities on the goals and level of learning that have been identified for that student. In this way, it is possible to individualize the mainstream experience for students as needed.

ACADEMIC SKILL DEVELOPMENT

Finally, it is important to note that mainstream courses present a major opportunity for mildly handicapped students to develop basic academic skills. Special education teachers and regular teachers can utilize this opportunity by embedding within the academic task structure instruction in and chances to practice (1) listening skills, (2) comprehension of written matter, (3) written expression, and (4) problem-solving skills. Students whose abilities are at the lower end of the developmental continuum benefit from skill instruction in the regular classrooms because they require direct instruction, more-than-average opportunities to practice, and a structure in which to generalize their skills from training situations to functional usage.

There are many steps teachers can take to improve students' oral comprehension of subject matter (listening skills). They should present highly organized lectures and summarize ideas at the end. Teachers can cue students to important information with statements like "It is important for you to know," "Please take this down in your notebook," and "Pay special attention because I may ask this on your test." Lectures should include some repetition, pauses to allow note-taking, and visual supplements, such as use of blackboard, overhead projector, and lesson outlines. Teachers should ask students to rate the comprehensibility of their lectures and make adjustments to their presentations several times during a semester (2, 16).

Teachers can help students improve their comprehension of written material by instructing them to read for various purposes. They may read slowly and underline for comprehension of main ideas, read italicized material and surrounding text to prepare for class discussions, and skim headings to prepare class assignments (3). Teachers may work in a small group format during which students and teacher take shared responsibility for processing text, finding information, and making notes (18). Slowly, the shared responsibility is shifted to students until they take independent control of the academic task. In other situations, teachers may rewrite and reorganize materials, identify supplementary material on a simpler level (3), highlight key words and phrases, and provide summaries, questions, and vocabulary lists. The time involved in preparing these aids calls attention to the need for collaboration among special and regular teachers.

Written expression is another skill that students must practice in order to improve. Because students with mild handicaps often fail to pay attention to the needs of the reader, they should be encouraged to consider their audience, identify the reasons for writing, and select content by its impact on the reader (8). They should learn to develop a plan for what they intend to say and to continue the planning process into the actual writing phase (8). Teachers may provide a model by demonstrating how *they* would ask themselves questions, clarify ideas, and organize and express their thoughts. Teachers may also present a good model by entering into a written dialogue with students. This dialogue, which may be in the form of a journal, can be meaningful written communication on any subject, including course-related content (11). The written dialogue process for the purpose of rewriting and editing class papers can alleviate using class time for conferencing. In general, teachers should understand the role of direct instruction, effective modeling, and frequent opportunities to practice skills in the development of written expression by students with learning handicaps.

Students with learning difficulties may be slow to acquire the problem-solving skills that they need to make progress in mathematics and science. By teaching problem-solving strategies, regular teachers can help their students gain access to higher-level course content. For example, they may devise and teach multiple-step problem-solving techniques such as the following:

1. Read the problem and clarify ambiguous or unknown word meanings.
2. Identify the question that the problem requires you to answer.
3. Identify what is already known.
4. Identify what is unknown.
5. Assign letter name(s) to the unknown(s).
6. Compose a sentence to describe the relationships among known(s) and unknown(s).
7. Write the sentence (#6) as an equation.
8. Solve the equation to answer the question (#2).

Teachers can demonstrate problem-solving strategies by verbalizing the steps they would take and then working with their students to solve problems. The teacher gradually withdraws from the shared responsibility, and the students move toward independent problem solving. Mathematics and science teachers may also teach students to use aids such as a multiplication matrix, calculator, or computer to solve problems. In general, low-achieving students need direct instruction, opportunities for guided practice, aids to bypass areas of deficit, and a focus on functional applications of academic skills in order to develop essential skills.

At the present time students with mild learning handicaps are experiencing difficulties throughout their school career and into adulthood. Research indicates less-than-optimal outcomes for these students when they take regular courses, generally high dropout rates, and rather discouraging job-keeping abilities. Currently we have the knowledge and technology to improve the goal outcomes for students with learning difficulties. This chapter has focused on the progress educators have made in developing teaching strategies and support structures for students who are in mainstream classes. As regular teachers and special educators improve their collaborative skills and work to infuse the practices described here into their programs, students will have the support they need to turn their failures into a pattern of successes that will bring their goals and wishes within reach.

TIPS FOR TEACHERS

1. Assign seats to mildly handicapped students that offer clear access to you and good visual and auditory reception.
2. Develop a predictable class period schedule and use a variety of familiar activities.
3. When creating cooperative learning groups, place

students with mild handicaps in groups with members who are good facilitators.

4. Whenever possible, check that students who need monitoring have recorded assignments in their assignment notebooks.
5. Ask good note-takers to carbon their notes for students who have difficulty taking notes.
6. For multistep assignments, develop a system to check students' work at every level.
7. Assign students to study in pairs for tests.
8. Assign pairs of students to read aloud to each other those passages from literature and textbooks that are crucial to comprehension of content.

DISCUSSION QUESTIONS

1. You have just learned from a special education teacher that one of your students has been identified as mildly learning handicapped. In what areas would you expect to collaborate with the special education teacher to improve the student's performance in your classroom?
2. What are common characteristics of students with learning handicaps? How might these characteristics affect learning in your classroom?
3. What steps would you take to modify your instructional strategies and assignments for a student in one of your classes who reads and comprehends text at a rate significantly below that of his/her classmates?

REFERENCES

1. Alley, G., and Deshler, D. *Teaching the Learning Disabled Adolescent: Strategies and Methods.* Denver: Love, 1979.
2. Beirne-Smith, M. "A Systematic Approach for Teaching Notetaking Skills to Students with Mild Learning Handicaps." *Academic Therapy* 24, no. 4 (March 1989): 425–37.

3. Cheney, C. O. "The Systematic Adaptation of Instructional Materials and Techniques for Problem Learners." *Academic Therapy* 24, no. 4 (March 1989): 25–30.

4. Christenson, S. L.; Ysseldyke, J. E.; and Thurlow, M. L. "Critical Instructional Factors for Students with Mild Handicaps: An Integrative Review." *Remedial and Special Education* 10, no. 5 (September–October 1989): 21–31.

5. Doyle, W. "Classroom Tasks and Students' Abilities." In *Research on Teaching,* edited by P. L. Peterson and H. J. Walberg. Berkeley, Calif.: McCutcheon, 1979.

6. ERIC Digest #448. *Research to Practice: Lesson Structure.* Reston, Va.: Council for Exceptional Children, 1987.

7. Graham, S. "Teaching Basic Academic Skills to Learning Disabled Students: A Model of the Teaching-Learning Process." *Journal of Learning Disabilities* 18, no. 9 (November 1985): 528–34.

8. Graham, S., and Harris, K. R. "Improving Learning Disabled Students' Skills at Composing Essays: Self-Instructional Strategy Training." *Exceptional Children* 56, no. 3 (November 1989): 201–17.

9. Gregory, J. F.; Shanahan, T.; and Walberg, H. "Learning Disabled Tenth Graders in Mainstreamed Settings: A Descriptive Analysis." *Remedial and Special Education* 6, no. 4 (1985): 25–33.

10. Johnson, D. W., and Johnson, R. "Mainstreaming and Cooperative Learning Strategies." *Exceptional Children* 52, no. 6 (1986): 553–61.

11. Johnson, S. E., and Hoover, J. H. "Use Dialogue Journals with Secondary Learning Disabled Students." *Academic Therapy* 24, no. 4 (March 1989): 75–80.

12. Kavale, K. A., and Nye, C. "Parameters of Learning Disabilities in Achievement, Linguistic, Neuropsychological, and Social/Behavioral Domains." *Journal of Special Education* 19, no. 4 (1985–86): 443–58.

13. Rosenshine, B. V. "Content, Time, and Direct Instruction." In *Research on Teaching,* edited by P. L. Peterson and H. J. Walberg. Berkeley, Calif.: McCutcheon, 1979.

14. Seidenberg, P. L. *The High School–College Connection: A Guide for the Transition of Learning Disabled Students.* Position Paper Series: Document No. 4. Greenvale, N.Y.: Long Island University, Demonstration Model Transition Project, 1986.

15. Slavin, R. E. "When Does Cooperative Learning Increase Student Achievement? *Psychological Bulletin* 94 (1983): 429–45.

16. Smith, T., and Dowdy, C. A. "The Role of Study Skills in the Secondary Curriculum." *Academic Therapy* 24, no. 4 (March 1989): 479–90.

17. Spruill, J. A. "Learning Is Something We Do Together: A Study of Special Needs Students in Regular Classrooms." *Dissertation Abstracts International* 48 (1987): 900A.

18. Stone, C. A. "Improving the Effectiveness of Strategy Training for Learning Disabled Students: The Role of Communicational Dynamics." *Remedial and Special Education* 10, no. 1 (January–February 1989): 35–42.

19. Zigmond, N.; Kerr, M. M.; and Schaeffer, A. L. "Behavior Patterns of Learning Disabled Adolescents in High School Academic Classes." *Remedial and Special Education* 9, no. 2 (1988): 6–11.

20. Zigmond, N., and Thornton, H. S. "Learning Disabilities in Adolescents and Adults." In *Learning Disabilities: State of the Art and Practice,* edited by K. A. Kavale. Boston: College-Hill Press, 1988.

Chapter 5

MAINSTREAMING THE CHILD WITH A VISUAL IMPAIRMENT

by Loraine J. Spenciner

Loraine Spenciner helps us increase our understanding of the nature of a visual impairment and how it may affect the student's performance in the classroom. She describes factors that affect the way an individual uses vision. She also explains eligibility criteria for special education services under the Education for All Handicapped Children Act, P.L. 94–142, as well as eligibility for additional state and national services based on the legal definitions of blindness and low vision. Finally, she suggests general teaching strategies to use in the regular classroom and specific curriculum considerations for reading, language arts, science, and social studies, as well as additional readings and resources.

INTRODUCTION

Place: Brooks Central School
          Fran Houser's classroom 7:20 A.M.

Setting: A round table piled high with a new shipment of science textbooks, 18 empty desks, and 2 figures huddled over steaming coffee mugs.

A nervous voice continues, "Jane, I'm just beside myself. I don't know what to do. . . . Last night Dr. Stone caught up with me as I was leaving the building and said that I was going to be getting a new student today . . . AND SHE'S BLIND. How

82

will I ever manage a child who can't see?"

Many people, unfamiliar with visual impairments, assume that "being blind" means that an individual cannot see. Most persons who are "legally" blind are not totally blind in a functional sense, however. In fact, over 75 percent of blind people have some usable vision (1).

UNDERSTANDING FUNCTIONAL VISION

Individuals with visual impairments differ in terms of how much vision they have and how they use it. Many persons can see near objects and may read print material at close distances; others may have little usable vision except to distinguish large shadows.

The definition of a visual impairment included in the Education for All Handicapped Children Act (P.L. 94–142) focuses on a functional definition of vision rather than a strict physical, or visual acuity, definition to determine students' eligibility for special education services.

> *Visual impairment:* . . . even with correction, [an impairment which] adversely affects a child's educational performance. The term includes both partial seeing and blind children. (3, 121a.5, b.11)

This federal definition of visual impairment is reflected in most state laws and regulations regarding special educational services to students. Students are eligible to receive these services if the visual impairment "adversely affects" performance in the classroom. Thus, a student need not have a specific limited visual acuity to be eligible for special services.

For the classroom teacher, several factors are important in understanding visual performance. Children with visual impairments may be able to use their vision in varying degrees of *efficiency,* depending on (1) the type of visual impairment, (2) the degree of loss, (3) the age at onset of loss, and (4) psychological factors unique to the student.

The first important factor is the type of visual impairment. Some kinds of visual impairments involve a scotoma, or blind spot in the visual field. A blind spot may greatly reduce a student's visual field or may result in a "Swiss cheese" effect where much information is lost in the areas of the scotomas. Other eye conditions such as severe myopia (nearsightedness) may involve a general decrease in visual acuity with no scotomas. This type of visual impairment may affect the degree of visual loss.

This loss, known as visual acuity, may refer to either distance or near visual acuity, and it is the second important factor in understanding visual efficiency. Information concerning a child's near visual acuity and type of loss will be essential to the classroom teacher in determining the seating arrangement and the types of materials to use with the student.

The third factor, the age at onset of blindness or low vision, affects the way the student functions in the classroom. Students who have had some usable vision in the past, even though they may no longer, usually retain visual memories that aid in the development of subject area concepts.

Finally, psychological factors are important in the *functional* use of vision. For example, two students may have the same eye condition and similar visual acuities. Both students may be able to use a standard text on map skills with a magnifying lens; however, one student may find this a very difficult task to perform, while the other has little difficulty. Thus, the two students do not have the same visual "efficiency."

Three instructional approaches can assist students in the use of low vision (2). The first approach, visual stimulation instruction, is designed for students with a limited amount of vision; it may include learning to tell whether or not a light is on or following a moving object with the eye. The second approach, visual efficiency instruction, focuses on more involved use of vision, such as distinguishing outlines and some detail of objects.

The third approach, vision utilization instruction, includes techniques for maximal use of vision and involves environmental modifications and optical and nonoptical aids.

UNDERSTANDING VISUAL IMPAIRMENTS: THE CHILD WHO IS BLIND

Visual impairments are sometimes considered in terms of the degree of impairment or visual acuity and are divided into two broad categories: blindness and low vision. The distinction between blindness and low vision is important because eligibility for some services may depend on whether or not an individual meets the legal definition of blindness. For example, the American Printing House for the Blind (APH) registers all legally blind school-age children. These children are then eligible to receive educational materials from APH through federal funding.

> *Blindness:* Visual acuity of 20/200 or less in the better eye with corrective glasses or a visual field defect of less than 20 degrees in the better eye.

According to the legal definition, an individual may be considered blind either because of low visual acuity or because of a visual field limitation.

The first part of this definition describes visual acuity in terms of how far an individual can see (distance vision). This means that persons with 20/200 vision can see at 20 feet what persons with "normal" vision can see at 200 feet. The definition describes visual acuity in terms of how an individual can see objects at a distance; it does not describe near visual functioning. Information about distance vision may be important when planning large-group activities or considering safety precautions on the playground. Can the child see the swing set area—or might s/he wander by without noticing another child swinging forward into the line of travel?

Yet for school-age children, information regarding near

vision is equally important in planning appropriate classroom activities. A teacher will want to ask specific questions about how the student functions in the classroom. Can the child see the blackboard from a seat in the first row? Can the child see a picture on the textbook page or printed words on handout materials? How much of the material should the child be expected to handle visually and how much should be presented orally or in a tactile format? School personnel can obtain information about general near visual functioning from the child's ophthalmologist. Specific information regarding classroom functioning, however, can be provided by a teacher or consultant with specific training in blindness and low vision.

The second part of the definition of blindness describes a narrow, restrictive visual field. Individuals who have field limitations of less than 20 degrees see objects clearly but through "a tunnel." Objects present outside this narrow field are not seen at all. Additional visual impairments may accompany a field loss so that a student may have limited acuity in addition to a restricted field. Specific information regarding the degree of loss should be discussed with the ophthalmologist. Questions concerning the implications of field limitations could be discussed with the teacher or consultant. For example, do we need to make modifications or material adaptations so that the student can participate in physical education activities involving fast-moving games such as softball or soccer?

Questions may also arise around another area. Some blind students exhibit mannerisms, or "blindisms," that are strange or disturbing to teachers and to the children's classmates. These behaviors may include eye poking, rocking the body back and forth, hand waving, or gazing at a bright light. Various explanations have been offered to explain "blindisms"; these habits seem to grow out of a need for self-stimulation, however (4). "The best approach is probably to keep the child involved in varied, interesting activities—especially activities using the hands. The child should not be punished or embarrassed in front of classmates if mannerisms occur, but may be quietly reminded of them" (p. 26). Direct teaching of alternative activities also has been found to be effective in decreasing blindisms (5).

In addition to understanding the physical aspects, it is important to consider some beliefs about blindness. Some of these common beliefs are simply overgeneralizations or myths (6). For example, many people believe that blind individuals are talented musically. The reality is that some blind people are very musical; others are not. Likewise, some blind people have an acute sense of hearing or touch; others do not. For many blind individuals, increased proficiency in the other senses may have come only after long years of direct instruction and practice.

Tips for Teachers on Understanding Blindness

Students who are *congenitally* blind have been blind since birth. Students who are *adventitiously* blind have had at least some vision during their early years before the onset of blindness. These students may continue to have some visual memories.

There is a difference between *functional* blindness and *legal* blindness. Two students may be *legally* blind with similar eye conditions and similar visual acuities. One student, however, may use the residual vision to a much fuller degree than the other. The first student may prefer to use print material although the material must be held a few inches away from the face. S/he may choose to read a print text over listening to the taped version. The second student may prefer to listen to most printed material or to receive a braille hard copy. Individual differences should be appreciated and respected.

Students who are totally blind, or who have too little vision to read print, are taught to read and write using braille. Special teachers, such as an itinerant teacher or consultant of students with visual impairments, usually provide this instruction. The braille system consists of a set of raised dots for each letter of the alphabet. Unlike our standard alphabet, however, the braille system also includes a type of "shorthand" or contractions. For example, the letters "EA" are combined into one braille symbol so that in words that contain the two letters together, only one braille symbol is written. In addition, some entire words are contracted so that a single braille letter stands for a whole word. There is also a special form of braille for mathematics, music, science, and foreign languages.

Suggestions for Further Reading About Blindness

Kastein, Shulamith; Spaulding, Isabelle; and Scharf, Battia. *Raising the Young Blind Child.* New York: Human Sciences Press, 1980.

Scholl, Geraldine T. *Foundations of Education for Blind and Visually Handicapped Children and Youth.* New York: American Foundation for the Blind, 1986.

UNDERSTANDING VISUAL IMPAIRMENTS: THE CHILD WITH LOW VISION

Educational services under P.L. 94–142 are provided for all students with visual impairments without distinguishing between those who are blind and those who have low vision. For students with low vision, however, eligibility for additional services from some state and national agencies may depend on meeting the legal definition of low vision.

Low Vision: Visual acuity better than 20/200 but less than 20/70 in the better eye with correction.

Tips for Teachers on Understanding Low Vision

Students with low vision usually experience a fluctuation in their visual functioning. Tasks that presented little difficulty last week may be more difficult this week. Unless the eye disorder is progressive, this fluctuation is usually temporary.

Suggestions for Further Reading About Low Vision

Jose, Randall T. *Understanding Low Vision.* New York: American Foundation for the Blind, 1983.

Scholl, Geraldine T. *Foundations of Education for Blind and Visually Handicapped Children and Youth.* New York: American Foundation for the Blind, 1986.

Sullivan, Martha G. *Understanding Children Who Are Partially Seeing: A Classroom Teacher's Guide.* Seattle: Special Child Publications, 1974.

TEACHING STRATEGIES FOR STUDENTS WHO ARE BLIND OR WHO HAVE LOW VISION

Some general considerations to keep in mind when working with students with visual impairments apply across grade levels and curriculum areas. They include the following:

1. Adopt a positive approach.

A teacher's attitude toward the student often sets the example for other students' reactions to that student. Treat the student with a visual impairment naturally, just as you would any other child. Don't avoid using words such as "see" or "look." The student will probably enjoy telling you about the program she or he "watched" on TV last night!

Blind students, like most students, tend to incorporate the attitudes of those about them. They live up (or down) to the expectations of those individuals. Educators should be aware of the influence that they maintain over students and be alert to ways that encourage students to be capable and independent.

2. Encourage independence through independent travel.

A special instructor with training in orientation and mobility will probably work with your student to become more familiar with the school environment; however, you can also assist the student to become physically independent in moving about the classroom as well as around the school. Several helpful ways relate to *classroom design.*

- Furniture in your classroom should be arranged so that

there is a clear path from the door into the room. A single piece of furniture in the direct line of traffic should be avoided.

- Chairs should be pushed under tables or desks when not in use.
- The location of furniture should be consistent from day to day. A wastebasket should not be placed on one side of your desk one day, and on the other side the next day.
- When items are changed in the room, allow the student to explore the new setup.
- For younger students, materials and equipment should be identified with tactile or visual symbols to assist them in independent identification.

School corridors should also be considered when creating a safe environment for independent travel.

- The corridor wall should be kept free of movable objects when possible. Since your student may use a "trailing" technique along the side of the corridor wall, unexpected objects will cause a collision.
- Classroom doors that open out into the corridor should be kept closed or completely opened.

When the child is first becoming acquainted with the school environment, a classmate may be assigned as a partner to assist the student in traveling from place to place. Once mobility skills have been gained, however, the student should be encouraged to travel independently. Assigning a sighted aide who is constantly with the student decreases self-esteem and self-confidence.

3. Learn how to be a sighted guide.

There may be times when your student will need to depend on a sighted person as a guide. You may want to know how to be a sighted guide, as well as how to train students in this method. The correct procedure is to have the student touch your elbow and walk slightly behind you and to your side. The student will be able to tell from your position when there are steps to climb or when you are turning a corner. A sighted guide does *not push or pull* the student along or *lead* the student by the arm or hand.

4. Interpret classroom events.

There are several ways in which you can assist your student in being an active member of the class:

- When writing on an overhead transparency or when using the chalkboard, it is helpful to say the words or figures as you write them. This assists the student in following along with the rest of the class.
- When introducing a new word, be sure to spell it aloud as you write it on the board.
- When explaining new concepts, try to link the new ideas to concrete experiences with which the student is familiar. Remember that many common experiences may not be in the student's repertoire. For example, the blind student may have only a limited conceptualization of the size and shape of some household pets.
- Avoid words such as "this" and "that" when possible; their meaning is difficult to interpret.
- Use descriptive language to interpret events that involve gestures or facial expressions. Students will spend less time in off-task behaviors or daydreaming when they are included in ongoing events.

5. Provide special materials for writing.

Students who are braille writers should have their own brailler (a small machine about the size of a portable typewriter) on the desk for ready use in doing written assignments. Older students may also use a slate and stylus or "paperless" braille-based computer system for note-taking. Some of these materials are available through the American Printing House for the Blind.

Students who are print writers often find that felt-tipped markers are easier to use than pencils or pens. Markers with various degrees of writing width provide a clear visual contrast between print and paper. Some students may need to be very close to their work; most students will find the writing position that is most comfortable for them.

Word processing programs are also important tools for writing. If the student is a print reader, a monitor that provides a high contrast is important. Monitors that display amber text on a black background are often preferred because of the good contrast that this color combination provides. Some students may also prefer to have enlarged letters such as 40- or 20-column format. Many word processing programs used in schools come with a 40-column option. Some programs, such as Magic Slate (published by Sunburst), also come with a 20-column option and a large print option for the printer.

The addition of a speech synthesizer card inserted into the computer allows both blind students and students with low vision to have access to word processing through speech as well as text. Speech synthesizers and software programs with speech output are available from a variety of regular educational sources as well as from the American Printing House for the Blind.

Another type of assistive technology, such as a refreshable braille device, allows the student to use a braille keyboard to enter text. The text is then read on a small display strip consisting of movable pins that are raised through a small grid and allow 20 to 24 braille characters to be read at one time. The braille student can either print a hard copy (print version) for the teacher, or, if a braille printer is available, can obtain a hard copy in braille.

Word processing has become an equalizer for many students with visual impairments. Editing and rewriting are extremely tedious tasks. The need to work up close to the paper often results in smudged writing, and copying is extremely time-consuming. Word processing facilitates the writing process and allows the student to complete written tasks in a timely fashion similar to their nondisabled peers.

6. Provide special materials for reading.

If your student is or will be a braille reader, specialized instruction in braille will be provided by an itinerant teacher or consultant. There are a few general suggestions to consider, however.

- Be sure to allow adequate time for students to complete reading assignments. Some students may need a little extra time for locating their materials and finding the starting place.
- You will probably want to vary the reading medium occasionally. Both braille and print readers may welcome a change by using taped materials or records.
- Students who are print readers will need to have text material that provides a clear, sharp contrast between text and page, as well as adequate spacing between lines. For some students, books with large print may be preferable; however, for most students these special books may provide an additional handicap. One effect of enlarging print is that it spreads the text, cutting down on the number of characters that the reader can see in a single glance. The result is a decrease in reading speed.

7. Provide special materials for science and social studies.

Several excellent modules have been developed for both the physical and the biological sciences. The Science Activities for the Visually Impaired (SAVI) project includes materials that can be used in the regular classroom by all students.

The Social Science Education Consortium has developed an equally useful set of materials for the social studies curriculum entitled *Social Studies for the Visually Impaired Child*. References to both sets of materials are included in the next section.

Suggestions for Further Reading About Program Planning

Awad, M. Michael, and Wise, Joe L. "Mainstreaming Visually Handicapped Students in Mathematics Classes." *Mathematics Teacher* 77 (September 1984): 438–41.

Billings, Gilbert W.; Cuphome, Elaine; and Nober, Linda W. "Lighting Up Science for the Visually Impaired." *Science Teacher* 47, no. 3 (March 1980): 28–29.

Bradley-Johnson, Sharon. *Psychoeducational Assessment of Visually Impaired and Blind Students—Infancy Through High School.* Austin: Pro-Ed, 1986.

Froschl, Merle; Colon, Linda; Rubin, Ellen; and Sprung, Barbara. "Including All of Us: Learning About Visual Impairment." *Day Care and Early Education* 14, no. 4 (Summer 1987): 24–31.

Hadary, Doris E., and Cohen, Susan H. *Laboratory Science and Art for Blind, Deaf, and Emotionally Disturbed Children.* Baltimore: University Park Press, 1978.

Mangold, Sally S., ed. *A Teachers' Guide to the Special Educational Needs of Blind and Visually Handicapped Children.* New York: American Foundation for the Blind, 1982.

SAVI/SELPH Program. *Activity Modules.* Berkeley, Calif.: Center for Multisensory Learning, Lawrence Hall of Sciences, University of California, 1981.

Singleton, Laurel R. *Social Studies for the Visually Impaired Child. MAVIS Sourcebook 4.* Boulder, Colo.: Social Science Education Consortium, 1980.

SUCCESSFUL MAINSTREAMING

Successful mainstreaming depends on the teacher's awareness that students with visual impairments can be independent, productive students in the regular classroom. In addition to local school personnel and regional teachers and consultants for students with visual impairments, there are organizations available to help in creating a successful school experience. Some of these agencies are listed below.

Additional Resources About Visual Impairments

American Foundation for the Blind
15 West 16th Street
New York, NY 10011

This national organization provides general information services, publishes material, and provides catalogs on various aids for persons with visual impairments.

American Printing House for the Blind
1839 Frankfort Avenue
P.O. Box 6085
Louisville, KY 40206

This publishing house is a major distributor of educational materials for students with visual impairments.

Helen Keller National Center for Deaf-Blind Youths and Adults
11 Middle Neck Road
Sands Point, NY 11050

This national center includes regional offices throughout the United States that provide technical assistance to education and training programs for older students and adults.

International Association of Lions Clubs
300 22nd Street
Oak Brook, IL 60570

Local community Lions Clubs are service organizations with a major interest in children and adults with visual impairments.

Library of Congress
1291 Taylor Street, N.W.
Washington, D.C. 20542

This national resource has regional lending libraries that house special reading materials, including cassettes and talking books.

National Association for Parents of the Visually Impaired
3329 Northaven Road
Dallas, TX 75229

This group provides support for families.

Recording for the Blind
215 East Fifty-eighth Street
New York, NY 10022

This organization lends taped educational books at no charge to students with visual or physical disabilities.

DISCUSSION QUESTIONS

1. How are specialized services provided to children with visual impairments in your state?
2. What common everyday experiences would be more difficult to interpret without vision? What would be some possible solutions? (For example, Everyday experience: Telling the difference between a one-dollar and a five-dollar bill. Solution: Fold each denomination in a different way.)
3. How would you describe a rainbow to a blind student?

REFERENCES

1. American Foundation for the Blind. *Facts About Blindness.* New York: the Foundation, n.d.
2. Corn, Anne L. "Low Vision and Visual Efficiency." In *Foundations of Education for Blind and Visually Handicapped Children and Youth,*

edited by Geraldine T. Scholl. New York: American Foundation for the Blind, 1986.

3. Department of Health, Education and Welfare. "Implementation of Part B of the Education for the Handicapped Act." *Federal Register* 42 (163) (August 23, 1977): 42490.

4. Orlansky, Michael D. *Mainstreaming the Visually Impaired Child: Blind and Partially Sighted Students in the Regular Classroom.* Austin: Learning Concepts, 1977.

5. Raver, Sharon A., and Dwyer, Robert C. "Using a Substitute Activity to Eliminate Eye-poking in a 3-Year Old Visually Impaired Child in the Classroom." *Exceptional Child* 33, no. 1 (March 1986): 65–72.

6. Scholl, Geraldine T. *Foundations of Education for Blind and Visually Handicapped Children and Youth.* New York: American Foundation for the Blind, 1986.

Chapter 6

STUDENTS WITH HEARING IMPAIRMENTS

by Toni Rees

Like children with visual handicaps, children with hearing disorders require special consideration. Toni Rees discusses several issues for educators to consider when working with students who do not hear normally. After defining terms, she explores communication challenges, legal rights, and responsibilities, and gives tips from teachers of mainstreamed children who are hearing impaired. She also includes a list of resources that offer avenues for further thought and exploration.

I know an expert fisherman who, every summer, takes his canoe and camper fishing in the lakes of northern Maine. When he is not working on another building project, testifying as an expert witness before the legislature, running a youth camp, keeping the books for a social club, or serving as a chairman of two nonprofit organizations, he is holding down his full-time professional job. He communicates using American Sign Language and does not speak. He is deaf.

Sometimes, as educators, we focus first on the disability and lose sight of the individual. A hearing impairment can be an isolating condition, a medical abnormality when viewed from the hearing person's perspective. Deaf people have been called an invisible minority, ignored or considered "dumb." In the past, children with hearing impairments were segregated in special schools, often in remote locations. Now, the majority attend public schools near their homes.

Talking about THE deaf child makes it seem as if the condition of being unable to hear normally transforms children into a homogeneous group. Children and adults with hearing impairments have diverse needs, personalities, and learning styles. Some students need the support provided by a day or residential program for deaf students. Others can succeed in their local public school with an interpreter, aide, and note-takers provided; some can be fully mainstreamed in regular classes with only a responsible adult to monitor auditory equipment and the learning environment.

"HEARING IMPAIRMENT"— WHAT DOES IT MEAN?

"Hearing impairment" is a generic term used to describe all degrees of hearing loss. Someone who is mildly hard of hearing may be called hearing impaired and so might the person who is profoundly deaf. A simple general distinction between someone who is "hard of hearing" versus "deaf" is that the hard-of-hearing individual may have difficulty hearing, but understands speech through listening, with or without the use of a hearing aid. The deaf individual has a hearing loss that precludes the understanding of speech through listening alone, with or without the use of a hearing aid (9). A further cultural definition of Deaf with a capital "D" refers to persons who perceive themselves as culturally deaf, meaning that they identify themselves as members of the deaf community and take pride in deaf culture.

The age at which hearing is lost has an important impact on learning and communication. A baby born deaf is said to have a congenital hearing impairment, meaning a hearing loss originating from birth. A child with a prelingual hearing loss is usually said to have lost the ability to hear by age three or before the time of well-developed language. A postlingual hearing impairment refers to a hearing loss occurring after the age of about three. The child who heard and acquired language and speech before becoming deaf has a great linguistic advantage over most children who are born deaf.

COMMUNICATION CHALLENGES

The process of acquiring a spoken language is very difficult for a child who cannot hear normally. At most, only 40 percent of English is visible on the lips, so speech reading is very ambiguous. In the past, a great deal of energy was expended on the controversy over whether to educate a hearing-impaired child using only speaking and listening (oral approach), or to combine speaking and listening with visual cues such as signing in English or Cued Speech (total communication approach). A third approach uses American Sign Language as the major language of instruction, particularly with young deaf children, and phases in the use of English after fluency has been attained in a primary language (bilingual/bicultural approach). Whichever approach is chosen, a hearing-impaired child needs a clear means of communicating.

There is a tremendous difference between a child who is hard of hearing and one who is deaf. A hard-of-hearing child typically develops communication skills through auditory chan-nels, by listening. Language acquired through hearing and speech is the natural means of expression for these children. Ross (11) estimates that there are in excess of 30 children per 1,000 with educationally significant hearing losses. These hearing impair-ments may be very slight, but affect the child's ability to understand and share in classroom activities.

Teaching a child who is hard of hearing is similar to teaching a child who can hear. To be successful, however, educators must consider the effects of hearing loss and the child's listening environment on the developing child. Well-maintained hearing aids and other amplification equipment used ap-propriately by students and teachers permit hard-of hearing, and even some severely hearing-impaired, children to function well in public school classrooms.

Teaching a child who is deaf is a very different proposition from teaching a child who can hear. To be successful with deaf children, educators must be aware of how to educate a hearing or hard-of-hearing child and additionally learn about visual aids or other means of communicating, as well as linguistic, social, and cultural considerations.

For a deaf child who is a fluent signer, English will probably be a second language. The public school educator who works with only one or two hearing-impaired children in an entire school district may find it helpful to consult a text on teaching English as a second language.

It is essential that all students be able to (1) communicate and (2) think. Hearing babies are bathed with language from the moment of birth. If children with hearing impairments do not have similar exposure to consistent and intelligible language, their development will inevitably be delayed.

Whatever the theoretical bases for difficulties, practitioners ask, "If the hearing-impaired child has a delay or disorder in language or thinking, what are the implications for the classroom teacher?"

1. Supplement and expand the child's experiences. Most parents of hearing-impaired children protect and limit their child's explorations of the world and social interactions for fear the child will be hurt. "No" and "can't," without explanations, feature large in the life of hearing-impaired children who do not hear road traffic noise, or dogs growling, or engines running, and who do not overhear and join in conversations about everyday events. It is sometimes helpful to think of the deaf student as a foreign student from another culture. The student who is deaf is likely to have many gaps in the understanding of expectations and routines. These gaps or deficits are not due to deafness per se,

but to inappropriate responses that have failed to prepare the child to cope with the normal experiences of everyday living.

2. Ensure the means for fluent, two-way communication. How to achieve fluent, two-way communication will depend on the needs of the child. For example, a child who is hard of hearing may need appropriate hearing aids in proper working order in a reasonably quiet environment. On the other hand, a child who is profoundly deaf may need the intervention of an interpreter.

3. A third implication of a language delay or disorder is the provision of appropriate language intervention strategies. This is the hardest area for the nonspecialist.

A speech/language pathologist should evaluate a child with a language problem and plan an appropriate language development program depending on the student's cognitive and developmental stage and needs. It is absolutely necessary that language development be integrated into the curriculum. Language is functional. Children will be motivated, will want to learn and improve their language use if they feel the power of language. Language is a tool to use for thinking, expressing, and understanding. It is not a set of computer drills or the imitation of the speech of an adult model.

LEAST RESTRICTIVE ENVIRONMENT

The decision about what constitutes a least restrictive environment for a particular child can only be determined after the Pupil Evaluation Team (PET) has convened and developed an Individualized Education Plan (IEP). The IEP must address the particular characteristics of a child and design the components of an appropriate education based on individual needs. After that process, the PET can determine what kind of educational setting will provide the component parts. It is NOT appropriate to first identify an educational setting that is readily available, and to then design an appropriate program. The educational program designed by the PET must dictate the setting, not the other way around.

In 1987, the president and the Congress commissioned a report on the education of children with hearing impairments. The Commission found that, of deaf children mainstreamed in public schools, only about half actually experienced any true integration, even on a part-time basis. They found that public schools lacked an understanding of the nature and diversity of hearing impairment. Consequently, deaf children's communicative, linguistic, and social needs were seldom met (14). This echoes the views of many deaf adults whose primary language is American Sign Language. These adults see special schools for children who are deaf as the least restrictive environments and view mainstreaming as more restrictive and socially isolating (3).

The Commission on Education of the Deaf advised educators to pay careful attention to a wide range of factors before determining the least restrictive environment for a deaf child. The Commission's report stated that the following must be considered when placement decisions are being made:

1. Academic achievement. The students in the class receiving the child with the hearing impairment must be functioning at approximately the same level as the child with the hearing loss.

2. Social development. The student with the hearing impairment must be functioning socially at a level similar to that of other students in the class. In order for this child to develop healthy self-esteem, the other students should be of a similar age (within two or three years) and should be capable of appropriate social interactions, both during class time and after school. Enabling the student to interact with adult hearing-impaired role models is also important. Some children who are deaf, who have never met adults who are deaf, reportedly believe that they will

die before reaching maturity or that children who are deaf grow into hearing adults.

3. Placement preference. The setting in which the student wants to learn, as well as the parents' wishes, must be considered.

4. Severity of hearing loss. What is the severity of hearing loss and the child's potential for using residual hearing? What are the child's programmatic needs for amplification and auditory training?

5. Communication needs. Does the child communicate primarily by listening and speaking or by using a more visual mode?

6. Emotional needs. Will the child's emotional needs be best met by living at home with parents or with age peers in a residential setting?

7. Linguistic needs. Does the student need a consistent, highly structured linguistic environment, or would interaction with individuals using a variety of linguistic styles be more appropriate? (14, pp. 21–23)

TIPS FOR TEACHERS

Academic goals and objectives are emphasized and obvious in school, but equally important for a successful and happy life are social and emotional growth goals. Educators play a vital role in the development of both.

As a teacher, what steps can you take to help the student with a hearing loss succeed in the regular classroom?

The prospect of dealing with a child who cannot communicate directly and easily with hearing people is unnerving for many educators. Added to that barrier is the necessity of working with technical auditory equipment and sometimes with esoteric signing systems. It is not surprising that educators often focus first on the difficulties, the disability, and lose sight of the individual.

This section discusses two main areas : (1) educational programming and developing or maintaining a positive climate in classrooms and schools, and (2) communication tips, including encouraging language development and speech, as well as working cooperatively with interpreters in the classroom.

Educational Programming

The foundation for academic success should be clearly defined in a child's IEP. The IEP helps a student who is exceptional keep as close to the school curriculum as possible. It should not serve to isolate a child. Ask yourself what curriculum outcomes you want for all students in your class. To achieve these outcomes for a hearing-impaired child, it is necessary to plan how to tie the IEP goals and objectives to the regular curriculum. You can help the hearing-impaired child by

- using alternatives to talking or lecturing for the introduction of concepts via visual approaches, as well as speaking; for example, use captioned films and overheads.
- previewing and reviewing material with the class and making sure the student understands. It is too easy and tempting for the student to nod, "Yes, I understand."
- providing enrichment activities. Children with hearing impairments do not easily overhear and acquire general knowledge from the television, radio, and conversation. It may even be helpful to think of students from other countries or cultures and ask yourself what they might not realize or know, and then apply a similar test to students with hearing impairments.
- discussing the best seating with the student. Not the back of the room! But immediately in front of the

teacher may be too close, like sitting in the very front seat at the movies.

- working in small, collaborative groups with academic, as well as collaborative, social goals.
- assigning a willing peer to assist the student with a hearing loss adjust to classroom routines.
- designating a note-taker for subjects that require one. Dual-sheet duplicating pads or old-fashioned carbon paper may be provided by the school. (Remember, the brightest student will probably take the fewest notes and so will not be the best note-taker for a student with a hearing impairment.)

Determining placement follows an analysis of a student's programmatic needs. However, a student with a hearing impairment who is, on paper, ideally suited for education in the mainstream will probably fail unless teachers and peers have positive and supportive attitudes. The mechanics of preparing to receive a student with a hearing impairment may be achieved by hiring interpreters, assigning note-takers and providing them with self-carbon note-taking pads, designating a person as responsible for questions about amplifying equipment, and designing an appropriate educational program in cooperation with the parents. To encourage success, all school staff need to be prepared to work with children who do not hear normally.

Most children pick up the rules of social interaction with only a little adult intervention. Children find a place among friends in school and, later, in the community at large. Children with a hearing impairment may need much more guidance and encouragement from school personnel to develop friendships and a sense of belonging in the mainstream classroom. Another way to foster both academic and social development is to provide opportunities for cooperative, small group project work. Mixed ability groups learn to share and divide responsibility. For example, a social studies project may entail groups of five or six children studying the local fishing community. Each member of the group is responsible for researching and presenting information. The depth of research and sophistication of the methods of presenting information will vary, but students must interact to produce an integrated whole.

Schools rarely seek input from the deaf community and yet deaf adults have a great deal to teach educators in public schools. Someone from the deaf community can be invited to the school to present information and answer questions on a staff development day. The nearest state school for deaf children, state department of education, bureau of rehabilitation, or university should be able to help locate an appropriate contact person. A deaf adult may be found to teach sign language. This can bring the double benefit of an improved self-concept for the deaf student and the ability to socialize with hearing students who are learning to sign.

The Commission on Education of the Deaf recognized the existence of an identifiable and important deaf culture and suggested that this culture be tapped by educators to help deaf students understand and cope with their deafness. The commission report stated that the psychological and social aspects of deafness need to be incorporated into school curricula and that

> they must not be suppressed in a misguided effort to deny the differences inherent in deafness. There is nothing wrong with being deaf. The sooner children realize this, the sooner they will fashion for themselves lives of achievement and excellence. (14)

Communication Tips

An educational reality is that students learn best when they actively participate. Hearing-impaired students need encouragement to volunteer information, work with others on projects, and discuss ideas. Teacher lectures are among the least effective means to learning for them. Instead of language lessons with instruction about syntax, give these children opportunities to use language in daily interactions. For example, as a teacher, I made extensive use of role playing and play writing in "English Language" classes. Children's attention focused on communicating meaning, rather than on the form of English sentences. The outcome was that children wanted and needed to practice grammatically correct English in order to attain the objective of the role-playing situation.

In an elementary school where I taught, children who were deaf were expected to read at least one book every week at home with someone in their family. Parents who were too busy were asked to encourage a brother, sister, grandmother, or friend to listen and talk with the child about the stories. Talking with a child does not mean asking direct questions, such as "Where did John go?" or "What did John do?" but rather to engage in conversation about some aspect of the book at whatever level the child is able to communicate.

A teacher can best help the child with a hearing impairment by making sure that

- both the teacher and the student's peers know how to communicate clearly. That includes facing the student when speaking, talking clearly, and rephrasing, not just repeating the same words, when the student does not understand.
- assignments are given both orally and in writing, to avoid confusion.
- films used in a darkened room are captioned, or that a light is on the interpreter's or teacher's face when he or she is explaining what is happening.
- each lecture starts with an outline of material to be covered in that period. At the end of class, key points are summarized.
- in class discussion, the person who is talking is signaled

so that the hearing-impaired student knows where to look. If an auditory trainer is in use, passing the microphone to the speaker is a way to signal who is talking and gives the hearing-impaired student a chance to follow and be part of the discussion.

A speech/language clinician cannot single-handedly provide effective speech and auditory training for a hearing-impaired child. Many hearing-impaired children are pulled out of the classroom for speech therapy; but to develop a skill successfully, it must be practiced and carried over into the broader school context. If you have ever taken a class as an adult in any subject—oil painting, karate, or preparing income-tax forms—you will know that for every hour of in-class instruction, several hours of practice are necessary in order to develop skills. The same principle applies to speech and language training. Isolated pullout therapy sessions will have little or no effect unless the student practices developing skills. The speech/language clinician needs sufficient tact and understanding to work in cooperation with classroom teachers to jointly plan reinforcement activities appropriate for each student.

There are several ways school administrators and nonspecialist teachers can work with speech/language clinicians to improve listening conditions in their schools. One way is to find someone who can explain in everyday functional terms the severity of a child's hearing loss and what the loss means. Do not be satisfied with an explanation that says Mary has a 50 percent loss. That tells you little or nothing. What you need to know is how much speech Mary understands and what conditions must exist in order for her to understand it.

Almost all hearing-impaired children could benefit from using amplification. Although a hearing aid makes sound louder, it does not fix damaged hearing. Increasing sound does not necessarily make sound clearer. Children who are deaf and hard of hearing hear differently. Teachers can help students to make the best of their residual hearing by ensuring that

109

- appropriate amplification is used; usually this means auditory trainers or individual hearing aids. Older children probably know exactly how to operate any specialized equipment and can help a teacher feel comfortable with it, too. Operating an auditory trainer is no more complex than turning on and adjusting a television. Doing either one properly takes a little practice before it becomes automatic.
- when talking to a class, they make sure that the student, or the student's microphone, is near them. The optimal distance between microphone and voice is only six inches.
- classroom noise is kept down when they are talking with students.
- hearing aids and auditory systems are checked daily.
- a professional person is appointed to oversee the student's hearing management program.

The school may have to contract with an audiologist or other knowledgeable professional to conduct in-service training for school personnel. Educators who work closely with children with hearing impairments must know (1) what equipment can and cannot do, (2) when to use the equipment, and (3) how to do simple troubleshooting checks to make sure the equipment is working properly every day. Educators also need to know what is reasonable to expect the student with the hearing impairment to understand, and what conditions have to exist in order for the child to understand.

Hearing aids and auditory trainers are commonly used by children with hearing losses. Neither can enable all children to hear clearly. Using a hearing aid does not cure a hearing loss in the way that eyeglasses enable many people to see. Why? Because if a child's inner ear is damaged, no matter how loudly sounds are amplified, the ear may not be able to distinguish between different sounds.

A hearing aid amplifies, or makes louder, all nearby sounds. For example, if the student is sitting next to an air-conditioning system, that sound will be amplified far more than the sound of the teacher's voice 15 feet away. For small group work, a personal hearing aid may enable some hearing-impaired children to follow and join in discussions. In a quiet room, a hearing aid may enable a child to pick up sound accurately at distances of about six to ten feet. Farther away, or in noisy conditions, an auditory trainer should be used. The speaker, usually the teacher, wears a radio microphone, and the student wears a receiving unit. It may be helpful to think of the microphone as part of a CB unit. Voices, coughs, and sneezes are all amplified and transmitted to the student. When a teacher leaves the classroom wearing a switched-on microphone, he or she is still broadcasting to the student from the teacher's room, the bathroom, wherever the microphone happens to be in the school.

A sound level meter can be used to test the noise level in a normal, busy elementary school classroom. A 60-decibel level is common. A teacher's voice instructing children is also commonly at 60 decibels. With normal hearing, it is possible to pull the teacher's voice out of the background noise and comprehend instructions. Using a hearing aid, noise will be amplified, distortion of sound occurs, and even a student with a mild hearing loss is unlikely to fully understand the teacher's speech in noisy classroom conditions.

Reducing classroom noise to an ideal level is expensive. Reducing classroom noise to a level where students with hearing impairments can at least function effectively can be cheap. Take some time to do an inventory of sources of noise. If possible, do the same inventory again, wearing a hearing aid. Is the hum of a failing fluorescent light magnified to an irritating level? Does sitting next to a noisy radiator make you jump? Is noise from outside the window suddenly a distraction? Brainstorm with other educators, students, and the school maintenance staff to reduce noise. Some simple solutions include the following:

- placing a carpet remnant in the hall outside the classroom to reduce the noise from footsteps.
- gluing small pieces of carpeting to the bottoms of the legs of chairs and desks to reduce the noise from chairs and desks scraping on a bare floor.
- using acoustic tile on the walls or cloth wall hangings or decorated egg cartons to absorb sound and make a better acoustical environment.

Working with interpreters in the classroom is increasingly common in public schools. If a child who is deaf is unable to make satisfactory educational progress by listening, speech reading, and talking, the PET may recommend using an interpreter. The team will have to evaluate the child's strengths and weaknesses and consider the parents' and student's preferences before a decision is made to hire an interpreter who uses Cued Speech, American Sign Language, or a form of signing that uses English grammatical structures.

For the first week or so, an interpreter is novelty entertainment for hearing students and a strange experience for the teacher. The deaf student may not know how to handle the experience either. Ideally, only fully qualified interpreters who have been screened and certified by the Registry of Interpreters for the Deaf should be hired. If it is not possible to hire nationally certified interpreters, at least find out what training the interpreter has completed. The professionally trained interpreter will enable the student to receive what educators and peers are saying. Unfortunately, many school systems hire well-meaning people who know some sign language or some Cued Speech, but who are not trained as interpreters. This is like hiring someone who knows how to count to teach mathematics or someone who knows how to cook to teach home economics. Interpreting involves skills, techniques, and judgment that are not necessarily naturally acquired along with learning to sign.

You can best help the hearing-impaired student by

- ensuring that the PET defines the communication mode used by the hearing-impaired student and that the interpreter is skilled in using the same mode—for example, American Sign Language, Cued Speech, a system of manually coded English, oral interpreting.
- clarifying the intepreter's role. The sole duty of a professional interpreter is to facilitate communication among deaf and hearing people, whereas interpreter/aides and interpreter/tutors may have a variety of duties.
- talking directly to the student, even though he or she may be watching the interpreter instead of you.
- permitting only one person to speak at a time during group discussions. Neither the student nor the interpreter can follow several people speaking at once.
- writing unusual words or technical terms on the board and going over them with the interpreter before class.
- remembering that the interpreter is a few words behind the speaker. Give the interpreter time to finish so that the deaf student can ask questions or join in the discussion.
- not talking while giving handouts. The student who is deaf cannot look for papers and watch you and the interpreter at the same time.

Success in school encompasses both academic and social achievements. A hearing impairment makes communication difficult, but interactions outside the classroom are a vital part of education. Hearing peers pick up cues from the school climate as to whether the hearing-impaired student is a valued part of the school community. Assess your school. To enable students with hearing impairments to participate:

- Do sports coaches provide visual as well as auditory signals?

113

- Are announcements over the public address system posted on a particular bulletin board?
- Are written copies of the school play made available?
- Do teachers and hearing students make the effort necessary to interact with deaf students?
- Do educational expectations and personal goals challenge the hearing-impaired students in your school?

If the answer to some of these questions is negative, what is your role in encouraging change? What are the barriers that stand in your way? What resources do you need to accomplish positive change?

RESOURCES

The American dream of equal access and educational excellence is as valid for the hearing-impaired student as for any other citizen. Sometimes it is hard to envision the special student 10 or 20 years hence, struggling with a mortgage or rent, car payments, a spouse, a job, children, and a dog. In my experience working with deaf people, that is the adult norm. Children who have been seen as school failures have made a transition into adulthood and responsibility. Have these attributes suddenly popped up from nowhere? Or have we, in school, been unable to see the abilities because of the focus on disabilities?

Dangers of labeling have been well documented, yet still we label. The self-fulfilling prophecy of low expectations is well known. Can we try a leap of faith and help children work out their own visions and goals? All occupations include persons who are deaf. There are deaf architects, lawyers, professors, chief executive officers, welders, morticians, writers, and artists. The student with the hearing impairment who sees successful adult role models may dare to dream, and, with careful support, find public school a relevant challenge—not a lonely experience to be endured and ended as soon as possible.

Gallaudet University and the National Technical Institute for the Deaf are institutions of higher education specifically created to serve students with hearing impairments. Increasing postsecondary educational opportunities are opening on college and university campuses throughout the nation. Adult education programs, community and junior colleges, vocational-technical and career schools, four-year programs, universities and graduate programs are not only accepting hearing-impaired students, but also they are providing support services and personnel as required by law.

National resources that help provide information and referrals for local contacts in your state include the following:

- Alexander Graham Bell Association, 3417 Volta Place, N.W., Washington, DC 20007. Telephone: (202)–227–5220. Information on oral programs, training in the use of residual hearing, parent education, etc.
- Gallaudet University, Information Center on Deafness, 800 Florida Avenue, N.E., Washington, DC 20002. Telephone: 1–800–672–6720. Provides information relating to all aspects of deafness: educational programming, deaf culture, research, interpreting, American Sign Language, legal issues, postsecondary education, parent education, etc.
- National Association of the Deaf, 814 Thayer Avenue, Silver Spring, MD 20910. Telephone: (301)–587–1788. Information on issues of concern to deaf adults, their families and friends.
- National Technical Institute for the Deaf, One Lomb Memorial Drive, P.O. Box 9887, Rochester, NY 14623. Telephone: (716)–475–6313. Information on postsecondary training in technical fields.
- Registry of Interpreters of the Deaf, Suite #1107, Rockville, MD 20850. Telephone: (301)–279–0555. Information on interpreting issues—for example, training, evaluation, and certification.

Some recommended books are listed in the References. The perspective of educators is given by Luterman in *Deafness in Perspective* (7). The viewpoint of parents is presented by Ogden and Lipsett in *The Silent Garden* (10), and observations by the deaf community are offered by Jacobs in *A Deaf Adult Speaks Out* (3).

DISCUSSION QUESTIONS

1. A hard-of-hearing child has been mainstreamed into your fourth grade classroom. In order to meet the child's needs appropriately, how will you prepare (a) yourself, (b) hearing children, (c) school personnel, and (d) your classroom and other school facilities?
2. A profoundly deaf student is joining your ninth grade social studies class. What should you find out in order to be able to serve the student appropriately?
3. You are the homeroom teacher for a profoundly deaf student who has just moved to your school district. What problems do you foresee for the student? What steps can you take to help alleviate these difficulties?

REFERENCES

1. Hakuta, K. *Mirror of Language: The Debate on Bilingualism.* New York: Basic Books, 1985.
2. *Handicapped Students and Special Education.* Rosemont, Minn.: Data Research, Inc., 1988.
3. Jacobs, L. *A Deaf Adult Speaks Out.* Washington, D.C.: Gallaudet Press, 1974.
4. Kretschmer, R. R., and Kretschmer, L. W. *Language Development and Intervention with the Hearing Impaired.* Baltimore: University Park Press, 1984.
5. Levine, E. S. *The Ecology of Early Deafness.* New York: Columbia University Press, 1981.

6. Luetke-Stahlman, B. "Using Bilingual Instructional Models in Teaching Hearing-Impaired Students." *American Annals of the Deaf,* December 1983.

7. Luterman, D. M., ed. *Deafness in Perspective.* Boston: College-Hill Press, 1986.

8. Meadow, K. P. *Deafness and Child Development.* Berkeley/Los Angeles: University of California Press, 1980.

9. Moores, D. F. *Educating the Deaf: Psychology, Principles and Practices.* Boston: Houghton Mifflin, 1987.

10. Ogden, P. W., and Lipsett, S. *The Silent Garden.* New York: St. Martin's Press, 1982.

11. Ross, M. *Hard of Hearing Children in Regular Schools.* Englewood Cliffs, N.J.: Prentice-Hall, 1982.

12. Sanders, D. A. *Aural Rehabilitation: A Management Model.* Englewood Cliffs, N.J.: Prentice-Hall, 1982.

13. Schildroth, A. N., and Karchmer, M. A., eds. *Deaf Children in America.* Boston: College-Hill Press, 1986.

14. *Toward Equality: Education of the Deaf.* Report to the President and the Congress of the United States. Commission on Education of the Deaf. Washington, D.C.: Government Printing Office, February 1988.

Chapter 7

TEACHING STUDENTS WITH SEVERE DISABILITIES IN THE REGULAR CLASSROOM

by Joanne W. Putnam

> *In this chapter, Joanne Putnam discusses the education of students with severe disabilities in regular classes. In the first section she introduces important issues surrounding the integration of students with severe disabilities in regular classes, providing a brief rationale for educational integration. The second section covers instructional and curricular approaches and presents tips for teachers. The final section discusses teacher collaboration and staff support needed to accommodate students with severe disabilities in regular classes.*

Born with cerebral palsy, impaired speech, and control of only his left leg, Irish writer Christy Brown struggled for recognition as a thinking, feeling person. The highly acclaimed film *My Left Foot* dramatizes Brown's accomplishments and his lifelong fight against prejudice. This story is a gripping one because of what seems to be an almost insoluble conflict between his mind and body, and audiences acutely feel the pain of devaluing and prejudicial treatment.

Christy Brown was a unique individual. But so too is every person with a severe handicap, although few are as talented and motivated as he. Nevertheless, within the disabled body is a sentient human who deserves the opportunity to develop to her or his full potential.

Americans like perfection and generally are uncomfortable when confronted with people who are less than perfect. The picture of classrooms that most teachers start out with does not include children who are misshapen or low in vision, or who wear heavy braces or hearing aids. Reality often takes some getting used to, but teachers all over the world find that it is one of the first principles of practicing their profession.

The uneasiness regular classroom teachers experience when confronted with the potential of having a student with severe disabilities placed in their classrooms is due to a number of factors. Teachers have indicated that (a) they do not feel adequately prepared to teach students with intensive needs; (b) the student's presence in the classroom might impede the achievement of nondisabled students; (c) meeting the students' management needs (such as toileting, using adaptive equipment) will pose problems; and (d) they fear adequate personnel and material supports needed to accommodate a student with severe disability will not be forthcoming.

Regular class settings are advantageous for students with severe disabilities in that they provide contexts in which (a) normalized peer interactions can occur; (b) typical models for appropriate behavior can be observed; (c) natural cues and correction procedures are likely to be used; and (d) friendships with nondisabled children can develop. Furthermore, when nondisabled students get to know severely disabled peers, they may be motivated to become potential future employers, good neighbors, and close friends (27). Also, and perhaps more important, regular class placement does not rule out for students with severe disabilities supplemental community-based instruction, the delivery of therapies, and appropriate individualized and unique programs. Finally, it is recognized that there will be some students with severe disabilities for whom the regular classroom may not be the most appropriate, least restrictive setting, but this decision must be made on an individual basis.

119

DEFINING INTEGRATION

Integration is a word that has come to mean many things and to take many forms, from lowering ethnic barriers to mainstreaming handicapped students; from the establishment of special classes for students with severe disabilities on a regular school campus to full programmatic integration of disabled and nondisabled students in academic classroom activities. As used here, educational integration refers to at least three types of inclusion: physical, social, and programmatic. Physical integration is the placement of students with disabilities in physical proximity to nondisabled peers. Social integration refers to situations in which disabled and nondisabled individuals have the opportunity to interact with each other. Programmatic integration permits disabled and nondisabled students to participate jointly in educational activities. The degree to which a student with severe handicaps becomes involved in academic activities depends, in part, on his/her instructional goals and objectives. At the minimum, all children, with and without disabilities, should have opportunities for meaningful interactions of reasonable duration that lead to perceiving a child as more than a handicap and as a full member of the classroom. The term "full inclusion" is being used currently to describe the provision of appropriate educational services and the meaningful inclusion of students with severe disabilities in regular classes.

THE NEED FOR STRUCTURED INTEGRATION ACTIVITIES

When students with severe handicaps are integrated, the nondisabled students' attitudes and social interactions are either positive or negative; the determinants are whether systematic intervention and modification of "typical" educational procedures have taken place (see Johnson and Meyer [21]). When special programs or interventions are not provided, the outcomes generally are not positive.

Studies of the effects of placing students with mild disabilities (e.g., learning disabilities and mild mental retardation) in regular classes indicate that these students tend to be more socially isolated and less socially accepted than their nondisabled peers (1, 9, 15). Voeltz (37) considered the negative outcomes associated with the physical integration of handicapped children simply to indicate the need for intervention; it is as appropriate for educators and other practitioners to address this need as it would be to address any other curricular need. Indeed, when systematic integration attempts are made, the results appear to be more positive and to show improved social interactions between disabled and nondisabled students, improved attitudes toward disabled persons in general, and improved student achievement (6, 20, 26, 30).

THE CURRICULUM

For students in need of special education services, the law (P.L. 94–142) requires an Individualized Education Plan (IEP) that contains annual goals and short-term objectives. If it is determined that students require additional specialized supports and services, their particular needs are to be assessed by a multidisciplinary team of professionals. An IEP sets forth educational goals, objectives, and needed services, and it must specify where and by whom the services will be provided.

Functionality and a Futures Orientation

Typically, students with severe disabilities require training in skills that are geared toward reinforcing those skills and activities that enable them to participate either partially or fully in integrated "current" and "future" environments (8). The skills and behaviors taught enhance the students' functioning in (a) school or vocational environments; (b) domestic environments (e.g., home); (c) community environments (e.g., the grocery store); and (d) leisure/recreation environments (e.g., a movie theater). The major portion of the curriculum for students with severe disabilities includes training in practical or functional skills, such as making purchases in stores, preparing meals, or carrying out self-care activities.

It is suggested that a school or school district provide teachers and parents with curriculum guidelines geared to preparing students for adult living. Owing to the relatively long time it takes for students with severe disabilities to acquire skills, it is important to address first the critical life skills to promote maximum participation in community environments. At the minimum, therefore, the curriculum should incorporate the following areas: (a) physical well-being, (b) independent living, (c) meaningful work, (d) financial support, (e) family living, (f) social and emotional well-being, and (g) recreation/leisure (3).

COMMUNITY-BASED TRAINING

To facilitate the acquisition of functional and social skills, students with severe disabilities should have a broad set of educational experiences, including community-based instruction. These students have difficulty generalizing what they have learned in one setting to another setting (e.g., from the classroom to the home, community, leisure, or work environment); hence skills should be learned in the same environments in which they are likely be used. For a portion of the school day, students with severe disabilities typically will spend time learning skills in such nonschool settings as restaurants, stores, laundromats, or offices.

The amount of time devoted to community-based instruction relative to school instruction should vary according to each student's needs. Sailor et al. in their "Community Intensive Instruction Model" (31) recommend increasing the amount of time spent in the community as the student ages. Thus, 3- to 8-year-old students should participate in the community once a week; 9- to 11-year-olds, twice a week; 12- to 18-year-olds, four times a week; and 19- to 22-year-olds, up to 80 percent–100 percent of the day.

Unfortunately, time spent in the community creates conflicts. Students have fewer opportunities for experiences in regular class and school activities and social interaction with peers, observational learning opportunities, participation in the class curriculum, and other learning experiences. The relative importance of school versus nonschool learning environments has yet to be determined empirically. It appears that certain tasks are learned best in the community and that other behaviors, especially those that involve social interaction, are best learned in classroom settings. Both types of environments are perceived as necessary contexts for essential learning.

CURRICULAR ADAPTATIONS

A critical goal for students with disabilities in regular classes is to gain access to the curriculum, or to participate in the same curricular activities as do regular education students. A special education curriculum should be linked to the regular education curriculum and, at the same time, take into account the unique needs of students with disabilities. Students with severe disabilities typically learn at a slower rate than do their nondisabled classmates, so lesson content expectations must be adjusted (a) to prevent a mismatch between lesson demands and a student's skill level; and (b) to assure the student's success in learning important skills.

Adaptations in the regular curriculum include (a) modifying student-response methods (pointing rather than responding verbally), (b) reducing the complexity of the curriculum objective (lowering the number of problems to be completed), (c) lowering the grade level of the curriculum (working on readiness skills while nondisabled students work on higher grade-level math skills), and (d) teaching a unique but related curriculum that may emphasize functional skills rather than academic skills (4).

Curricular adaptations will likely require students with disabilities to learn individually as well as in small or large groups. Individualized instruction can take place outside the classroom for brief periods; however, to enhance the benefits of regular class participation, it is recommended that students receive in-class instruction to the maximum extent possible. Porter (29) recommended that a student with disabilities leave the regular class for specialized instruction to meet the student's needs only for "compelling" reasons. If individualized instruction must take place, it should occur somewhere in the classroom. For example, specialized material or equipment (e.g., a computer or an electronic communication device) may be placed in the rear of the classroom for a teacher's aide to use when assisting in instructional delivery.

Given the focus of this chapter, participation in regular classes, strategies to promote inclusion in ongoing class curricular activities are pertinent. Giangreco and Putnam (13) describe two broad options for curricular adaptations: (a) multilevel curriculum selection and (b) curriculum overlapping.

Multilevel curriculum selection refers to engaging nondisabled and disabled students in an activity in the same subject area or curricular domain, but varying the expectations for achievement according to the ability level of the student with disabilities (10). For example, nondisabled students in a second grade class may engage in writing a story about dinosaurs while the student with severe disabilities traces the letters of the word "dinosaur" or a picture of a dinosaur. Another example is taken from a bilingual school district in Canada: students in a secondary-level French class are expected to write compositions in French and the student with severe disabilities is expected to use French vocabulary words to verbally identify three picture cards.

By using the levels provided by Bloom's *Taxonomy of*

Educational Objectives (5), teachers can individualize student objectives in a particular subject area according to the different "levels" of learning: knowledge, comprehension, application, analysis, synthesis, and evaluation. Although it is unlikely that students with severe cognitive disabilities could accomplish learning objectives at the analytic or synthesis levels, they should be able to perform well at the knowledge level (e.g., identifying tools) or the comprehension level (e.g., understanding uses of tools).

Students with disabilities may not have a chance to interact with peers if their objectives require learning activities that are too disparate from the activities specified for the rest of the class. To avoid isolating the student with severe disabilities, teachers should structure peer interaction activities. For example, a peer tutor might guide the student in identifying sight words. (Peer interaction activities are discussed later in this chapter.)

Curriculum overlapping refers to activities in which students with and without disabilities work together in groups, although their instructional objectives are generated from different curricular areas. For example, in a group geology project to simulate a volcanic eruption, a student with severe disabilities could participate with the following instructional objectives: (a) greet fellow students; (b) assist in constructing a papier-mâché volcano by pasting on strips of paper; (c) identify the colors of the paints used; and (d) increase verbalizations to peers.

Partial Participation. If it is unreasonable to expect students with severe disabilities to participate fully in academic activities with their nondisabled peers, every effort should be made to enable them "to function, at least in part, in a wide variety of least restrictive school and nonschool environments" (2). Partial participation (e.g., in the geology lesson) is highly compatible with curriculum overlapping and multilevel curricular strategies.

ENHANCING PEER INTERACTIONS

A number of approaches exist for structuring social situations to maximize positive interactions between students with severe disabilities and their nondisabled peers. Thousand and Villa (35) underscore the importance of instructional practices that use "peer power," a "key variable in meeting the needs of a diverse student population within the regular education setting" (p. 6). Such practices include cooperative learning, peer tutoring, peer buddies/special friends, and peer support groups.

Cooperative Learning

Over two decades of research have demonstrated that cooperatively structured activities are more beneficial than individualistic or competitive activities in promoting positive cross-handicap social interaction behaviors. In cooperative groups individuals work together to reach common goals, in contrast to learning situations in which an individual's goal attainment is not correlated with group-goal attainment (individualistic) or is negatively correlated with others' goal attainments (competitive).

Johnson, Johnson, and Holubec (19) have conceptualized the cooperative learning teaching strategy as consisting of six basic elements:

1. The accomplishment of a group goal is dependent upon positive interdependence, or group members working together to achieve the group goal. Methods for promoting positive interdependence are (a) setting mutual goals for group members (goal interdependence); (b) structuring divisions of labor (task interdependence); (c) dividing and/or sharing materials, resources, or information among group members; (d) assigning students to different roles (role interdepend-

ence); and (e) giving joint rewards (reward interdependence).

2. Face-to-face, verbal (or other communication forms) interactions must occur.

3. Students are held individually accountable for mastering the assigned material and contributing to the group's efforts.

4. Students are expected to employ positive interpersonal and small-group skills. Teachers provide direct instruction on how to collaborate in the groups (e.g., by instructing students in helping others to understand an assignment, active listening, or taking turns).

5. Teachers monitor student behavior during the activities and provide students with feedback during the group discussions after the cooperative lessons.

6. Students are also engaged in self-evaluation within the groups to discuss how well they functioned or met the learning objective.

Over 50 studies have been conducted on mainstreaming and cooperative learning. Johnson, Johnson, and Maruyama (20) and Johnson and Johnson (18) reviewed 41 studies comparing the relative effects of two or more goal structures on the interpersonal attraction between students with and without disabilities. Cooperative learning experiences produced greater interpersonal attraction between the two groups than did competitive and individualistic experiences. Cooperative learning experiences also have been found to "promote more differentiated, dynamic, and realistic views (and therefore less stereotypic and static views) of other students (including handicapped peers and students from different ethnic groups) than do competitive and individualistic learning experiences" (17, p. 115).

Although most studies of the efficacy of cooperative learning have involved students with mild disabilities, the application of such procedures to students with moderate and severe handicaps is increasing. Studies have been conducted in elementary and secondary schools and in recreation settings during activities as varied as science projects, art, cooking, music, academic and pre-academic tasks, and group recreation activities (12, 16, 22, 23, 30, 40). In general, these studies show that cooperative learning situations are associated with significantly higher levels of certain positive social and verbal interaction behaviors, greater interpersonal attraction, and greater academic gains, compared to those in competitive and individualistic situations.

The cooperative learning study by Putnam et al. (30) involved students with moderate and severe disabilities in a fifth grade science class. The purpose of the study was to compare the effects of cooperative skill instruction on the social behaviors of students. Students receiving the cooperative skill instruction interacted more positively with one another than those who did not receive this instruction. The cooperative learning method combined aspects of curriculum overlapping as well as partial and extended participation in the science activities (e.g., students with severe disabilities obtained the equipment from a table and poured water into a container during an experiment on displacement).

Peer Tutoring

Given proper guidance and preparation, nondisabled students have demonstrated the ability to facilitate the skill development of students with severe disabilities (7, 28). In peer tutoring programs, same-age or cross-age peers assume a role similar to that of teacher, using appropriate instructional procedures. The benefits of peer tutoring, which have been discussed by Kohl, Moses, and Stettner-Eaton (24), include an efficient, cost-effective way to increase the amount of individualized instruction available to tutees. Tutoring is a good way to prepare nondisabled children to accept and interact positively with persons who have disabilities. Students who are tutors benefit at least as much as the peers they tutor in terms of learning activities and learning levels of psychological maturity (34).

A potential disadvantage of peer-tutoring programs is the "hierarchical" relationship between tutor and tutee (27). That is, a tutor taking on the role of "instructor" or "helper" is seen as more competent. This relationship contrasts with the "horizontal" interactions that children most often experience with peers. In addition, little is known about the long-term effects of peer tutoring on relationships between students with and without disabilities (25).

An important aspect of making peer tutoring work well is adequate supervision by teachers and the serious commitment of time by staff members to the program. Sprinthall and Blum (34) recommended weekly seminars where teaching techniques can be discussed as well as methods of helping tutors to process their own experiences (see the curriculum guide developed by Sprinthall and Blum [34]) for examples of lesson topics for seminars).

Peer Buddies/Special Friends and Peer Support Networks

Peer buddies or special friends programs are unlike peer tutoring programs insofar as the goal for peers is to develop friendships and spend time together in social and leisure nonacademic activities. Peers may eat lunch together, walk together in the halls between classes, or participate together in after-school activities, such as attending a basketball game. Teachers can help students with and without disabilities to acquire the necessary social, play, and communication skills essential to interactions. A "special friends" trainer's manual has been developed and validated for use in integrated school environments (see Voeltz et al. [39]. Outcome studies on the special friends model show significant and positive attitudinal effects as a result of this program (38).

Peer support networks expand upon the peer buddy system to include a group of peers who work together to foster a sense of belonging and to enrich the life of the disabled student. Several peers strive to break down the social and educational barriers facing students with intensive needs. Also referred to as "support circles" (33), the members are committed to helping an individual lead a full and independent life. At least one member becomes a strong advocate for the "circled" person. All group members work toward empowering the challenged student to set goals and reach them, as well as fostering in that person a true sense of being wanted and needed.

TEACHING THE VALUE OF INDIVIDUAL DIFFERENCES

All students benefit from learning about and experiencing a broad range of individual differences. Systematic efforts can be made to integrate content about individual differences into the curriculum (e.g., creating a unit of instruction or diffusing information in different areas of the curriculum).

Teacher Modeling. Teachers can exert a strong influence on student attitudes toward peers with disabilities by their own actions and verbalizations. Teachers can present a positive example by treating the student with disabilities respectfully, as they do other students in the class, by (a) speaking to the student as they would to other students, not as if the student were a very young child; (b) not using labels or language concerning disabilities that sets the student apart from the rest of the class (e.g., not referring to the student as "our Down's or CP child"); and (c) modeling positive social interaction behaviors (e.g., initiating a conversation with a student using a communication board) (32).

Using Kid Power. Older and respected children or adolescents can also teach students about disabilities and positively affect attitudes. In an interesting article 10-year-old Amy Turnbull (36) describes a science project she conducted in a second grade classroom. The purpose of the study was to assess the effect of peers teaching students about mental retardation on students' attitudes toward people with mental retardation. The approach involved the following:

> I read a book about a boy who is mentally retarded, and I showed them a film about the Special Olympics. I also showed them my brother's Special Olympic medals. I asked the class questions, and they asked me questions. I told them that people who are mentally retarded learn slower than us. But they can still learn. I also said that brains are like a record player, because they work on different speeds. They learned that music is played on both slow and fast speeds. I told them that brains of kids with mental retardation work slowly and our brains work fast, but all of us can learn and have happy lives. (36, p. 44)

The results of this study indicated that pretest to posttest attitude score changes for students who received the instruction were significantly more positive than the scores of students who were not exposed to the instruction. Turnbull recommended that older students be used to teach younger students about disabilities inasmuch as the older children are able to use words, explanations, and interesting presentations that younger children will understand and relate to. Moreover it was observed that younger children are very likely to listen to and value the ideas presented by older peers who are liked.

When informing students about disabilities, caution should be used to avoid reinforcing perceptions of difference. This means not using labels or focusing on features that set the children with disabilities apart from others. Some emphasis should be placed on what students with disabilities have in common with others in the class, as well as on their special strengths and gifts.

TEACHER SUPPORT

Teacher Ownership. It is essential that the regular class teacher assume primary "ownership" and accept responsibility for the education of a student with disabilities, just as he/she does for all students on the class list. When a teacher feels responsibility for a student with disabilities, he or she is more likely to become involved with the student's educational program and to enjoy the rewards associated with the student's achievement of learning goals and the benefits accruing to the entire class. Without teacher ownership, it is likely that a student with disabilities will be socially and academically isolated from the rest of the class. However, regular class teachers already have substantial responsibilities in educating 20 to 30 nondisabled students. The addition of a student with severe disabilities to the classroom requires direct and immediate support from a specialist or consulting teacher with expertise in educating students with disabilities, and perhaps an aide.

Consulting Teachers. It is imperative that regular class teachers receive assistance from professionals with specialized skills in teaching students with severe disabilities. Such teachers are referred to by various titles (e.g., methods and resource teachers, special education consulting teachers, education specialists, collaborative consultants), and their participation is a crucial ingredient in the success of integration attempts (29). Addressing the need for teachers with specialized skills to fill these roles are teacher education programs at, for example, the University of Vermont, Western Oregon State College, and the University of Montana. Consulting teachers may serve one or several schools, a district, or a cooperative of school districts.

Teaming. A staffing model that emphasizes team teaching and teacher collaboration increases the potential for successful integration in regular classes. Teams can vary in size from two to six and may be composed of professionals who represent various disciplines and constituencies, including teachers, parents, students, peers, administrators, and specialized personnel (35).

Related Service Personnel. Specialists such as speech/language therapists, physical therapists, and occupational therapists also support the educational programs of students with severe disabilities, based on the needs specified in the students' IEPs. These services should be provided in a manner that is compatible with the regular education schedules or routines. It is recommended that whenever possible such services be delivered according to an "in class/consultative model" (14). When specialists provide consultative services, their recommendations are more likely to be incorporated into the student's daily routine; as a result, the skill is practiced more often in naturally occurring circumstances.

Paraprofessionals. Teacher aides or educational assistants play an important role in supporting students with severe disabilities in regular classes. Staffing patterns for paraprofessionals vary according to the following configurations: (a) assignment to one student on a full-time basis; (b) assignment to several students (a small group) within the same class or school; (c) assignment to students for part of the day and to other school duties (e.g., playground supervision) for another portion of the day; (d) assignment to a student (or several students) on a part-time basis.

Teacher aides can attend to many of the management needs of students with severe disabilities. Management needs refer to aspects of the educational program that are provided to the student to assure equal access to educational opportunities (13), such as repositioning for physical comfort, assisting in toileting, or providing adaptive devices or materials. Care must be taken to preserve student dignity and privacy when attending to management needs. In addition, some services will take place out of the regular class (e.g., administering medication in the health office). At times when teachers are unable to leave the class, teacher aides can provide invaluable assistance.

The role of the paraprofessional in assisting a student with disabilities should be clarified. Aides typically assist in instructional delivery, but are not involved in educational evaluation or development of goals and objectives and instructional decisions. Aides should not be expected to replace the teacher. The extent to which a teacher aide is involved with a student is an extremely important consideration. Too much time spent with one student (a) can result in staff "burnout"; (b) may impede natural interactions with other students; (c) may result in the student becoming overly dependent on the teacher aide; and (d) may detract from the regular class teacher's sense of "ownership" of the student with severe disabilities (13, 41). Moreover, funding a full-time teacher aide for one student may put an undue financial hardship on a school district.

Family Support. Families of students with disabilities play an essential role in the educational process and are key members of the educational team. Involving parents in the educational planning process for students requiring special education services is mandated by federal law (P.L. 94–142). Parents and family members are unique and especially valued members of the collaborative team, particularly because they have an understanding and historical perspective on their child that no one else possesses.

TIPS FOR REGULAR CLASS TEACHERS

The following are some practical strategies for integrating students with severe disabilities into regular classes based on the material presented in this chapter:

1. Place students in regular classes according to "natural proportions."
2. Emphasize functional skill training for participation in current and future environments.

3. Alter the curricular objectives for the student with severe disabilities by (a) reducing the complexity of the objective; (b) modifying student response methods or instructional approaches; or (c) developing unique instructional objectives.
4. Schedule time for community-based instruction.
5. Carefully structure peer interaction experiences, such as cooperative learning.
6. Directly teach all students collaborative skills.
7. Use peer tutors, peer buddies, and circles of friends to facilitate positive peer interactions.
8. Teach nondisabled students about individual differences as part of the class curriculum (emphasizing the giftedness of all students).
9. Assume primary responsibility for the education of the students with severe disabilities in your class.
10. Utilize consulting teachers, specialists with expertise in the education of students with severe disabilities, paraprofessionals, parents, and administrators to serve as members of the support team.
11. Team teach with the consulting teacher whenever possible.

CONCLUSION

Just as students with severe disabilities were the last group with disabilities to receive a free and appropriate public education, they will likely be the last group of students to be integrated into regular classes. Curiously, students with severe disabilities have been left out of the debate concerning the Regular Education Initiative. Although a number of schools and school districts in the United States and abroad are including students with severe disabilities into regular classes, so far most are not. Systematic evaluations of demonstration projects are beginning to appear in the literature, but the research data base on the effectiveness of various approaches and strategies for regular class placement is scant.

Dedication to human rights and human dignity has led to the national willingness to consider changing the past practices of segregating students with severe disabilities. Moreover, it is believed that benefits accrue to students with disabilities (e.g., opportunities for observing typical models and developing friendships) as well as to students without disabilities (understanding individual differences, opportunities to learn from peer tutoring, and the social/psychological rewards obtained when advocating for and helping others).

Many teachers, students of education, parents, and professionals are beginning to recognize that the techniques designed to promote the educational integration of students with severe disabilities (such as community-based instruction, multi-level curricular activities, cross-age tutoring, and support circles) are effective for nondisabled students as well. The process of building a society in which diverse individuals have an integrated and productive role begins in our schools. Ultimately, an appropriate education that addresses individual needs, fosters a sense of self-worth, and inculcates feelings of belonging is a fundamental goal for all students, whether they are or are not disabled.

RECOMMENDED READING

Biklen, D. *Achieving the Complete School: Effective Strategies for Mainstreaming.* New York: Teachers College Press, 1985.

Certo, N.; Haring, N.; and York, R., eds. *Integration of Severely Handicapped Students: National Issues and Progressive Alternatives.* Baltimore: Paul H. Brookes, 1984.

Forest, M., ed. *Education/Integration: A Collection of Readings on the Integration of Children with Mental Handicaps into Regular School Systems.* Downsview, Ont.: National Institute on Mental Retardation, 1984.

Forest, M., ed. *More Education/Integration: A Further Collection of Readings on the Integration of Children with Mental Handicaps into Regular School Systems.* Downsview, Ont.: G. Allan Roeher Institute, 1987.

Horner, R. H.; Meyer, L. H.; and Fredericks, B. H., eds. *Education of Learners with Severe Handicaps: Exemplary Service Strategies.* Baltimore: Paul H. Brookes, 1986.

Lipsky, D. K., and Gartner, A., eds. *Beyond Separate Education: Quality Education for All.* Baltimore: Paul H. Brookes, 1989.

Meyer, L. H.; Peck, C.; and Brown, L., eds. *Critical Issues in the Lives of Persons with Severe Disabilities.* Baltimore: Paul H. Brookes, in press.

Organizations

1. American Association on Mental Retardation
   1719 Kalorama Road, N.W.
   Washington, DC 20009 1–800–424–3688

2. Association for Persons with Severe Handicaps
   7010 Roosevelt Way, N.E.
   Seattle, WA 98115 (206)–523–8446

3. Council for Exceptional Children
   1920 Association Drive
   Reston, VA 22091 (703)–620–3660

4. National Down's Syndrome Congress
   1800 Dempster Street
   Park Ridge, IL 60068–1146 1–800–232–NDSC

DISCUSSION QUESTIONS

This chapter has presented a rationale for integrating students with severe disabilities into regular classes. Based on this material and your perceptions:

1. What are your predictions about future directions in educational integration?
2. What barriers exist to achieving full inclusion?
3. What are the advantages and disadvantages of integration for nondisabled students?

REFERENCES

1. Asher, S. R., and Taylor, A. R. "The Social Outcomes of Mainstreaming: Sociometric Assessment and Beyond." *Exceptional Education Quarterly* 1 (1981): 13–30.
2. Baumgart, D.; Brown, L.; Pumpian, I.; Nisbet, J.; Ford, A.; Sweet, M.; Messina, R.; and Schroeder, J. "Principle of Partial Participation and Individualized Adaptations in Educational Programs for Severely Handicapped Students." *Journal of the Association for the Severely Handicapped* 7, no. 4 (1982): 17–27.
3. "Best Practice Guidelines for Students with Intensive Educational Needs." Results of a survey of Vermont educators and parents. Pamphlet.
4. Bigge, J. *Curriculum-Based Instruction for Special Education Students.* Mountain View, Calif.: Mayfield Publishing Co., 1988.
5. Bloom, B. S. *Taxonomy of Educational Objectives, Handbook I: Cognitive Domain.* New York: David McKay Co., 1956.
6. Bricker, D. "A Rationale for the Integration of Handicapped and Nonhandicapped School Children." In *Early Intervention and the Integration of Handicapped and Nonhandicapped Children,* edited by M. J. Guralnick. Baltimore: University Park Press, 1978.
7. Brinker, R. P. "Interactions Between Severely Mentally Retarded Students and Other Students in Integrated and Segregated Public School Settings." *American Journal of Mental Deficiency* 89 (1985): 587–94.
8. Brown, L.; Nietupski, J.; and Hamre-Nietupski, S. "The Criterion of Ultimate Functioning and Public School Services for

Severely Handicapped Students." In *Hey, Don't Forget About Me: Education's Investment in the Severely, Profoundly, and Multiply Handicapped,* edited by M. A. Thomas, 2–15. Reston, Va.: Council for Exceptional Children, 1976.

9. Bryan, T. "Peer Popularity of Learning Disabled Children." *Journal of Learning Disabilities* 7 (1974): 621–25.

10. Campbell, C.; Campbell, S.; Collicott, J.; Perner, D.; and Stone, J. "Individualized Instruction." *Education New Brunswick–Journal of Education* 3 (June 1988): 17–20.

11. Davis, W. E., and McCaul, E. J. *New Perspectives on Education: A Review of the Issues and Implications of the Regular Education Initiative.* Orono, Maine: Institute for Research and Policy Analysis, University of Maine, 1988.

12. Eichinger, J. "Effects of Goal Structures on Social Interaction Between Elementary Level Nondisabled Students and Students with Severe Disabilities." *Exceptional Children,* forthcoming.

13. Giangreco, M. F., and Putnam, J. W. "Supporting the Education of Students with Severe Disabilities in Regular Education Environments." In *Critical Issues in the Lives of Persons with Severe Disabilities,* edited by L. H. Meyer, C. Peck, and L. Brown. Baltimore: Paul H. Brookes, in press.

14. Giangreco, M. F.; York, J.; and Rainforth, B. "Providing Related Services to Learners with Severe Handicaps in Educational Settings: Pursuing the Least Restrictive Option." *Pediatric Physical Therapy* 1 (1989): 55–63.

15. Gresham, F. M. "Misguided Mainstreaming: The Case for Social Skills Training with Handicapped Children." *Exceptional Children* 48 (1982): 422–33.

16. Jellison, J. A.; Brookes, B. H.; and Huck, A. M. "Structuring Small Groups and Music Reinforcement to Facilitate Positive Interactions and Acceptance of Severely Handicapped Students in the Regular Music Classroom." *Journal of Research in Music Education* 32 (1984): 243–64.

17. Johnson, D. W., and Johnson, R. T. *Cooperation in the Classroom.* Edina, Minn.: Interaction Books, 1984.

18. _____. "Cooperative Learning and Mainstreaming." In *Integration Strategies for Students with Handicaps,* edited by R. Gaylord-Ross, 233–48. Baltimore: Paul H. Brookes, 1989.

19. Johnson, D. W.; Johnson, R. T.; and Holubec, E. J. *Circles of Learning: Cooperation in the Classroom.* Rev. ed. Edina, Minn.:

Interaction Books, 1986.

20. Johnson, D. W.; Johnson, R. T.; and Maruyama, G. "Interdependence and Interpersonal Attraction Among Heterogeneous and Homogeneous Individuals: A Theoretical Formulation and a Meta-analysis of the Research." *Review of Educational Research* 53 (1983): 5–54.

21. Johnson, R. E., and Meyer, L. H. "Program Design and Research to Normalize Peer Interactions." In *Integrating Moderately and Severely Handicapped Learners: Strategies That Work,* edited by M. P. Brady and P. L. Gunter, 79–101. Springfield, Ill.: Charles C. Thomas, 1985.

22. Johnson, R. T.; Johnson, D. W.; DeWeerdt, N.; Lyons, V.; and Zaidman, B. "Integrating Severely Adaptively Handicapped Seventh-grade Students into Constructive Relationships with Nonhandicapped Peers in Science Class." *American Journal of Mental Deficiency* 87 (1983): 611–19.

23. Johnson, R. T.; Rynders, J.; Johnson, D. W.; Schmidt, B.; and Haider, S. "Interaction Between Handicapped and Nonhandicapped Teenagers as a Function of Situational Goal Structuring: Implications for Mainstreaming." *American Educational Research Journal* 16 (1979): 161–67.

24. Kohl, F. L.; Moses, L. G.; and Stettner-Eaton, B. A. "The Results of Teaching Fifth and Sixth Graders to Be Instructional Trainers with Severely Handicapped Students." *Journal of the Association for the Severely Handicapped* 8, no. 4 (1983): 32–40.

25. Krouse, J.; Gerber, M.; and Kauffman, J. "Peer Tutoring: Procedures, Promises, and Unresolved Issues." *Exceptional Education Quarterly* 1 (1981): 107–15.

26. Madden, N. A., and Slavin, R. E. "Mainstreaming Students with Mild Handicaps: Academic and Social Outcomes." *Review of Educational Research* 53 (1983): 519–69.

27. Meyer, L. H. "Why Integration, or Why NonHandicapped Kids Should Be Friends and Not Tutors." Paper presented at the 12th Annual Conference of the Association for Persons with Severe Handicaps, Boston, December 1985.

28. Meyer, L. H.; Fox, A.; Schermer, A.; Ketelsen, D.; Montan, N.; Maley, K.; and Cole, D. "The Effects of Teacher Intrusion on Social Play Interactions Between Children with Autism and Their Nonhandicapped Peers." *Journal of Autism and Developmental Disorders* 17 (1987): 315–32.

29. Porter, G. "School Integration, Districts 28 and 29." In *More Education/Integration*, edited by M. Forest. Downsview, Ont.: G. Allan Roeher Institute, 1987.

30. Putnam, J.; Rynders, J.; Johnson, R.; and Johnson, D. "Collaborative Skill Instruction for Promoting Positive Interactions Between Mentally Handicapped and Nonhandicapped Children." *Exceptional Children* 35, no. 6 (1989): 550–58.

31. Sailor, W.; Anderson, J. L.; Halvorsen, A. T.; Doering, K.; Filler, J.; and Goetz, L. *The Comprehensive Local School: Regular Education for All Students with Disabilities.* Baltimore: Paul H. Brookes, 1989.

32. Searl, S. J.; Ferguson, D. L.; and Biklen, D. "The Front Line—Teachers." In *Achieving the Complete School: Strategies for Effective Mainstreaming*, edited by D. Biklen, 52–103. New York: Teachers College Press, 1985.

33. Snow, J., and Forest, M. "Circles." In *More Education/Integration*, edited by M. Forest. Downsview, Ont.: G. Allan Roeher Institute, 1987.

34. Sprinthall, N. A., and Blum, L. T. "Peer and Cross-age Teaching: Promoting Social and Psychological Development in Mainstream Classes." In *Social Environment of the Schools*, edited by M. C. Reynolds. Reston, Va.: Council for Exceptional Children, 1980.

35. Thousand, J. S., and Villa, R. A. "Accommodating for Greater Student Variance in Local Schools." *International Journal of Special Education*, forthcoming.

36. Turnbull, A., and Bronicki, J. B. "Changing Second Graders' Attitudes Toward People with Mental Retardation: Using Kid Power." *Mental Retardation* 24, no. 1 (1988): 44–45.

37. Voeltz, L. M. "Program and Curriculum Innovations to Prepare Children for Integration." In *Public School Integration of Severely Handicapped Students: Rational Issues and Progressive Alternatives*, edited by N. Certo, N. Harring, and R. York, 155–83. Baltimore: Paul H. Brookes, 1984.

38. Voeltz, L. M., and Brennan, J. "Analysis of Interactions Between Nonhandicapped and Severely Handicapped Peers Using Multiple Measures." In *Perspectives and Progress in Mental Retardation. Vol. 2. Social, Psychological, and Educational Aspects*, edited by J. M. Berg, 61–72. Baltimore: University Park Press, 1984.

39. Voeltz, L. M.; Hemphill, N. J.; Brown, S.; Kishi, G.; Klein, R.; Freuhling, R.; Collie, J.; Lively, G.; and Kube, C. *The Special*

Friends Program: A Trainer's Manual for Integrated School Settings. Rev. ed. Honolulu: University of Hawaii, 1983.

40. Wilcox, J.; Sbardellati, E.; and Nevin, A. "Integrating a Severely Handicapped Girl in a First Grade Classroom with Cooperative Learning Groups." *Teaching Exceptional Children* 20, no. 1 (1987): 61–63.

41. York, J.; Vandercook, T.; Caughey, E.; and Heise-Neff, C. *Does an "Integration Facilitator" Facilitate Integration?* Minneapolis: University of Minnesota, December 1988.

Chapter 8

GIFTED STUDENTS IN REGULAR CLASSROOMS

by Susan B. Tarver and James A. Curry

Susan Tarver and James Curry address the opportunity for classroom teachers to participate in the identification of and programming for gifted students. They have divided the chapter into three major parts. The first part focuses on ways in which classroom teachers might recognize and help to identify gifted students through their classroom behaviors. The second part examines the use of specific strategies for modifying the regular curriculum so that it "matches" the identified needs of gifted learners. The third part describes management options for implementing learning experiences for gifted students.

INTRODUCTION

A major challenge facing teachers in regular classrooms is providing appropriate and sufficient curricula to diverse populations. Students display wide ranges of abilities, specialized learning needs, and learning styles. These academic attributes, coupled with family and environmental factors, contribute significantly to the uniqueness of students' needs, requiring teachers to modify their general curricula, instructional materials, and methods in order to help students develop their potential for achievement. Certainly exceptional students, whose needs may not be met sufficiently through the standard curriculum, are among the most challenging for teachers to serve.

Although in recent years much attention has focused on students with handicapping conditions, the attributes of another group of students also require the modification of general classroom curricula and instructional methods. Meeting the needs of students who show exceptional academic and/or creative ability, whose performance (or potential for performance) exceeds the capabilities of their classroom age-mates, requires teachers to adapt or to generate curricula that will provide such students with the opportunity to close the gap between their potential and their maximum levels of performance. These students, called "gifted" or "gifted/talented," often receive services in elementary schools through a resource room or a "pullout" setting (on a part-time basis) and in secondary schools through "honors" courses or electives. Since their exceptional abilities (which translate into exceptional needs) are with them all the time, those needs must also be addressed within the regular classroom and through the regular curriculum.

This chapter suggests ways in which teachers in elementary and secondary school classrooms may

- recognize gifted students through their classroom behaviors;
- adapt existing curricula to increase the level of academic and creative challenge provided for gifted students; and
- manage learning experiences for gifted students within a classroom structure.

RECOGNIZING GIFTED STUDENTS IN THE CLASSROOM

Research by Borland (1) and Gear (6) suggests that classroom teachers can be effective identifiers of gifted students. Key elements are training and information that provide teachers with an understanding of the specific kinds of positive and/or negative behaviors that gifted students may show in classroom settings. Lists of these students' common characteristics are not sufficiently concrete to assist classroom teachers in recognizing giftedness.

In using any list of characteristics and observable behaviors to determine which students show signs of giftedness, classroom teachers must consider three important points. First, a student's behavior or performance should be compared only to behaviors or levels of performance usually shown by his/her age peers. It is not possible to assess the degree to which a student is exceptionally able if his/her performance is being compared to that of an older student. The differing levels of social, emotional, and physical development will confuse the question, resulting in uncertain assessment.

Second, the misconception that gifted students always display their characteristics through positive behaviors has resulted in the failure of some teachers to recognize giftedness in certain children. Despite the overwhelmingly positive image that the word "gifted" conjures, gifted behavior is not exclusively positive or enjoyable for either the teacher or the student him/herself. Kaplan (7) and Curry (3) have emphasized that a student may show giftedness through behaviors that are enjoyable or exciting in the classroom (positive behaviors), or through behaviors that are disruptive or pose problems (negative behaviors). In an attempt to combat the myth of giftedness as a "heavenly" attribute, Richert et al. (12) have even developed a list called "Characteristics of the Gifted That Tend to Screen Them Out of Programs."

Third, teachers should not assume that a student is gifted if he/she possesses one or two characteristics; nor should they assume that a student is not gifted unless he/she possesses all the listed characteristics. Assuming the former is too *inclusive;* it is likely that many children in the class will show at least one characteristic on a checklist. Assuming the latter is too *exclusive;* it is unlikely that any child will show all the characteristics simultaneously. The key to observing students' behavior is to remember that the purpose is to assess educational need. The educational diagnosis of "gifted" should be made only when

- the intensity of a characteristic(s) or
- the combination of characteristics with other characteristics

indicates that the scope of the general curriculum—that which is provided for all children—will be too limited to assist a student to maximize his/her potential.

Figure 1 lists characteristics commonly associated with giftedness; it also provides examples of positive and negative classroom behaviors by which each characteristic might be recognized.

MODIFYING CURRICULA FOR GIFTED STUDENTS

Although a curriculum may be specially created for gifted students, most classroom teachers find teaching the amount of material contained in the general curriculum quite challenging enough. In fact, most teachers would surely resist a directive to develop a whole new curriculum for their few students whose learning traits may not be sufficiently challenged by the classroom's general curriculum. Utilizing strategies for extending existing curricular material is a more practical approach to meeting gifted students' needs within the structure of the regular classroom.

Kaplan (7), Curry (3), Maker (9), and others propose that general curricula be modified for gifted students by extending basic components shared by all learning experiences. This section suggests means by which the curricular components of *content, process,* and *product* may be appropriately adapted so that learning experiences will more nearly and consistently meet the

Figure 1
Characteristics and Behaviors of Giftedness

Common Characteristics	Positive Classroom Behaviors	Negative Classroom Behaviors
Learns more rapidly; retains information more easily and longer	• masters basic skills easily • early reader • precocious in mathematics • unusual academic achievement	• becomes bored • resists rote or repetitive tasks • disrupts class when work is finished
More curious, has a stronger need to know	• has large stores of information • prefers complexity	• asks *many* questions • gets "off topic" frequently
Independent thinker, has a questioning attitude	• is self-confident • expresses original opinions • is good at independent projects	• is rebellious, challenges authority • resists conformity to social norms
Superior abstract thinking ability	• is willing to consider unusual ideas • shows skill in problem solving	• resists conventional approaches/answers • presents arguments almost *too* well
Senses discrepancies	• is interested in current issues • is concerned with fairness, justice, "real" problems	• is a perfectionist • is critical of own and others' ideas
Intellectually playful	• is good risk taker (in areas of strength) • appreciates plays on words • has a sophisticated sense of humor	• interrupts with "humorous" distractions • gets carried away with jokes
Intense or more sophisticated interests	• shows high motivation/long attention span in interest area • has complex ideas/information in unusual areas	• may suffer from peer isolation • is a daydreamer • resists interruption when involved in interest area
Wide range of interests	• easily motivated in new areas • has many hobbies • is involved in many activities	• leaves projects unfinished • overextends him/herself
Superior and divergent communications ability	• has large vocabulary and accurate usage • shows flair for various means of expression (e.g., computer graphics, drama, cartooning)	• may be perceived as a "show-off" by peers and adults

Sources: Clark (2); Curry and Epley (4); Gallaher (5); Kaplan, Madsen, Gould, Platow, and Renzulli (8); Parke (10); and VanTassel-Baska and Strykowski (14).

147

needs of gifted students. By modifying one or more of these three components, teachers may develop learning experiences that will be both challenging to gifted students and integrated with existing classroom curricula.

Modifying Curricular Content

All learning experiences possess the element of content, or subject matter, for students to learn. Content may be *simple,* requiring that students learn the facts, rules, details, concepts, and generalizations that are basic to the subject area being taught. Content may also be *complex,* requiring that students extend their understanding to consider the issues (which are debatable), the problems (which are solvable), and the themes (which are multidisciplinary) that arise within the subject area.

The distinction between simple and complex content may be seen in examples from a unit on the presidents of the United States. Simple content in the general curriculum might include

Facts:	The powers of the president
Rules:	The legal requirements that all presidential candidates must satisfy
Details:	The accomplishments of particular presidents
Concept:	The role of the executive branch in the balance of power
Generalization:	The traditions that have been established and perpetuated through the office of the president.

Gifted students' abilities to learn rapidly and to retain information (and the fact that they often already possess great stores of information) indicate a frequent need for curricular extension beyond simple content. Increasing content complexity is one strategy teachers may use in adapting individual lessons (or entire units of study) to meet the needs of their exceptionally able students. Complex content for the unit on the presidents of the United States might include

148

Issue: Whether or not to retain the two-term limit
                currently imposed upon presidents
Problem: How to regulate campaign contributions so
                that candidates cannot be unduly influenced by
                large donors such as political action committees
Theme: The study of patterns of change as it relates to
                leadership.

Developing learning experiences that require gifted students to bring their knowledge of simple content to bear upon related broader issues, problems, or themes addresses their need to be both competent consumers of information as well as producers of information. It also responds to their heightened concern with solving "real" problems (11).

Modifying Curricular Process

All learning experiences possess the element of "process," or the thinking skills that students are asked to learn or to practice. Just as content may be simple or complex, process may be *basic* or *productive*. Although many models delineating levels of basic and productive thinking have been developed, "basic" cognitive processes are generally described as knowing, understanding, and using information or skills. These basic thought processes are used by students to master requisite information that will enable them to become effective adult participants in society. For example:

Knowing: • List unsafe situations that you might see on
                the playground.
                • List the major characters in the play *Romeo
                and Juliet.*
Understanding: • Explain why playground rules are important
                for children to know.
                • Describe the conflict between the Montague
                family and the Capulet family.

Using:
- Make a model that shows three things you might find on an unsafe playground.
- Act out an exchange between the friends of feuding families.

Basic thought processes are as crucial to gifted students as they are to all children. Learning experiences that focus exclusively on the use of basic process skills will be insufficient, however, if gifted students are to develop many of their learning potentials (including abstract thinking skills and independent thinking).

At the productive levels of process, students are asked to use creative thinking (to generate ideas) and critical thinking (to judge, verify, or dispute ideas). For example:

Creative:
- Design a new piece of playground equipment that is both safe and fun.
- Speculate on what other ways the prince might have stopped the feuding between the Capulets and the Montagues.

Critical:
- Decide which three playground rules are the most important to remember. Tell your reasons.
- Defend or dispute the right of Romeo and Juliet to marry one another without the knowledge or permission of their families.

By extending learning experiences from basic to abstract thinking skills, teachers increase the probability that gifted students will develop their propensities for generating and judging ideas and will respond in ways more closely reflecting their gifts.

Modifying Curricular Products

A third component of all learning experiences is the product element, or the ways in which students demonstrate what they have learned and share their ideas. Although "product" may call to mind some sort of concrete display, teachers may also use a variety of intangible means by which to learn about students' learnings and ideas. Kaplan (7) suggests four basic product categories: *written, visual, verbal,* and *kinesthetic.*

Teachers tend to provide students with many opportunities to learn and practice written product forms (e.g., tests, essays, stories, book reports, and worksheets) and, to a lesser degree, verbal product forms (e.g., debate, public speaking, mock interviewing, oral reports). Since facility with written/verbal forms of expression holds a crucial place in our society, such a concentration is understandable. However, written and verbal means of expression may not allow some students to present adequately the depth or complexity of the information they possess or the ideas they have generated.

Despite the central place that written expression holds in our society, other societal factors (such as extensive technological advancements) have expanded the role of verbal communication, and have increased the roles of visual and kinesthetic means of communication. For gifted students, these communications media may be better suited for sharing the complex, innovative nature of their ideas and their more sophisticated interests, and for developing more fully their divergent communication abilities. The use of diverse products may also assist in discovering "hidden" giftedness within students who, due to the limitations of written expression, have not had their potential recognized.

The purpose in establishing product categories is not to determine the single category into which a specific product falls, but rather to expand teachers' overall concept of "product." Though by no means an exhaustive list, Figure 2 provides a variety of means by which teachers might ask students to share information and ideas.

Figure 2
Curricular Product Options

WRITTEN

biography
book report
booklet
checklist
commercial
crossword puzzle
description
diary
dictionary
editorial
field manual
guidebook
handbook
letter
list
magazine
manual
notebook
poem
research report
test
worksheet

KINESTHETIC

apparatus
charades
dance
demonstration
dramatization
finger puppets
game
pantomime
papier-mâché
puppets
role play
signing

VERBAL

advertising jingle
characterization
commercial
debate
description
dialogue
interview
lecture/lesson
monologue
oral book report
panel discussion
recording
speech
storytelling

VISUAL

bulletin board
calendar
cartoon
chart
collage
display
drawing
flannel board
flow chart
graph
mobile
model
mural
painting
photo essay
picture dictionary
poster
puzzle
scrapbook
time line
videotape

Summary on Curriculum

In developing appropriate learning experiences for their gifted students, classroom teachers may modify one or more individual curricular components (i.e., content, process, and/or product). This differentiation of the general curriculum will address gifted students' unique learning characteristics, providing them with greater opportunities for developing their advanced abilities to the fullest degree.

MANAGING OPTIONS FOR GIFTED STUDENTS IN REGULAR CLASSROOMS

Although a wide variety of options is available and appropriate for classroom teachers of gifted students, three of those options are particularly effective: (1) gaining time for extension activities by modifying classroom assignments; (2) involving students in independent or small group studies; and (3) structuring differentiated assignments using learning centers or resource options.

Modifying Classroom Assignments

A concern often expressed by classroom teachers is that given gifted students' regular classroom assignments, they do not have the time to complete differentiated learning activities. At the same time, however, many gifted students may be required to complete assignments designed to "reinforce" information and skills that they have previously mastered. For example, students who are already able to spell and use the "new" spelling words correctly on the very day that the list is presented may still be held responsible for the four days' worth of spelling exercises that precede the spelling test. Similarly, able mathematics students are often required to complete the same number of practice problems as their classmates despite their early (or previous) mastery of the computational process involved.

By modifying gifted students' classroom assignments, by shortening or even excusing students from some basic assignments, teachers will find that time for more challenging extension activities will be available. For example, students whose mathematical abilities make it possible for them to complete a current unit more quickly than their classmates may use the regular period to devise and solve mathematical logic problems. Advanced spellers may be excused from spelling altogether and use their new-found time to investigate a particular area of interest (see the following section on independent/small group studies). These forms of acceleration are most easily utilized when the content being studied is sequential and when mastery can be objectively tested. By using commercially prepared or teacher-developed inventories of the knowledge and skills contained in the general curriculum, and by shortening or replacing unnecessary assignments for their gifted students, teachers will find that the question of time for differentiated activities becomes less critical.

Caution must be exercised so that such modifications do not result in gifted students lacking mastery of crucial basic material. Gaps in basic knowledge and skills will only place these students at risk later. With carefully selected inventories and regular documentation, however, teachers can be assured that gifted students will complete only those assignments that they legitimately need, and can use the time gained for more appropriately challenging curricular extensions.

Independent/Small Group Studies

As noted earlier, gifted students often possess a wide range of interests, a single intense interest, or an interest in investigating complex content areas. By establishing means through which students may pursue such interests, elementary and secondary classroom teachers may both challenge and motivate their gifted learners.

An in-class program of independent or small group study requires preparation prior to classroom initiation. Once developed, however, the program can partially run itself. Five basic steps are necessary: (1) determining the target group, (2) developing a management system, (3) introducing the system to targeted students, (4) establishing regular "checkpoint" meetings, and (5) involving others in the program.

1. *Determining the Target Group.* Although independent or small group study is an appropriate option for many gifted students, a classroom teacher just initiating such a program may decide to target self-directed students while waiting to involve others until the program has had at least one trial run. Students who finish their classwork consistently early, students who show intense interest(s) and high motivation, or students with excellent organizational skills and work habits may be those targeted for the program's first cycle. Once a teacher has become more comfortable with the system, and his/her role as facilitator, other gifted students (such as those who seem to be underachieving or whose organizational habits or classroom behaviors will require greater teacher involvement) may be invited to participate.

2. *Establishing a System.* A system of sequential assignments that will guide students through their studies should be established prior to initiating the program. For example, students may be asked to meet scheduled due dates for a series of activities such as identifying a topic, stating a problem to investigate, selecting a research design, gathering and analyzing information, and presenting findings (13). By developing materials such as project contracts, time line formats, and guide sheets, a classroom teacher can establish a system within which she/he facilitates the

projects but each student takes individual responsibility for completion of specific tasks.

3. *Introducing the System.* Before students begin independent or small group studies, concrete information should be shared in such areas as the way in which the overall system will operate, the kinds of topics open to investigation, the performance expectations, the impact upon "regular" classwork and report card grades, and whether participation in the project is mandatory or permissive. It is also essential that students be taught the requisite skills of research. Teachers may also want to inform the parents of students involved. For students, information may best be provided through a small group discussion or individual conferences. A letter or telephone call may be sufficient to inform parents of pertinent details and to answer questions.

4. *Establishing Checkpoints.* After starting the program, the teacher should meet regularly with each student (or small group of students) to determine progress, and establish or modify target dates for completion of each task. Project schedules can be varied to respond to aspects such as an individual student's abilities, project complexity, and access to resources. Limiting the number and scope of projects (at least in the program's initial cycle) will help the teacher to assess the ability of individual students to handle program tasks and to avoid becoming overburdened with students' needs for individual assistance. (Limiting the scope of projects will also keep some students from "getting in over their heads" through unrealistic goal setting.) Checkpoints may be quite brief (10 minutes) but should be regularly scheduled in order that students may maintain interest and continuity in their project work.

5. *Involving Others.* As soon as the teacher is reasonably comfortable with the program structure and its operation, other students and adults can become involved. By including other individuals (such as foster grandparents, student teachers, older students, and parent volunteers) in facilitating student projects, a teacher may feel freer to involve more students.

Although the target group for the program may be gifted students, some other students may have the motivation and ability to participate as well. Such a spillover effect can only be positive when the program's tasks are appropriately modified to reflect differing ability levels. Most students enjoy investigating new areas, and extra classroom time can be well spent on projects by those students whose abilities and classroom performance allow them the time to become involved.

Independent and small group studies are an excellent way in which teachers may both respond to gifted students' advanced levels of ability and intense interests, and provide curricular extension through the investigation of issues, problems, or themes.

Learning Centers and Resource Options

Many elementary teachers use learning centers in their classrooms. However, usage is often confined either to simple management of regular class assignments or to free-time activities. Centers may also be used to provide extension activities for students at different levels of ability.

For example, a learning center in an elementary school classroom may be developed to supplement a literature unit on American tall tales. The center should contain many resource materials, such as collections of tall tales, illustrations of famous

157

tall-tale heroes, and materials for making different kinds of products. The following types of activities might be included:

1. Meet with the other students in your group to list as many everyday situations as possible for which a tall tale might be invented. Compile your ideas into a booklet of writing ideas. Choose one situation from the list and write a tall tale or write and perform a skit.
2. Choose your favorite traditional tall tale, either from those you have read in your group or from others you have read on your own. Think about what would happen if that tall tale really happened in our town. Write a news release for the local newspaper or draw a cartoon.
3. Add a character from American history to an existing tall tale. Share what you think would happen in that tall tale by writing in a new piece of dialogue or illustrating a new action sequence that involves the character you have chosen.
4. Invent a tall tale in which your hero or heroine uses a really wild or unusual way to deal with a common, everyday problem. Share your new tall tale by telling it to a group of students.

These activities show that a unit from the general curriculum (tall tales) may be extended by requiring students to use both productive process levels and alternative product forms. For students whose exceptional abilities lie in the areas of reading and writing, the preceding activities would require more than the single class period often allocated to creative writing. Activities in the learning center may be teacher-assigned or student-selected after gifted students have shown their knowledge of basic information (e.g., the origin of American tall tales, general characteristics of tall tales, the specific traditional tall tales included in the unit).

Just as with independent small group studies, other students may also participate. Because of the time needed to acquire the basic unit information, other students may be able to complete fewer learning center activities. But the challenge of using productive thinking skills and communicating through alternative product forms is certainly crucial for all students to experience, even though the need is neither as urgent nor as frequent for them as it is for gifted students.

Resource options may be used by secondary teachers to adapt and extend the regular curriculum. The options may include (1) community mentor programs and internships; (2) computer-assisted instruction with data bases, simulations, and utility programs; (3) enrollment in college or university courses during the semester; (4) participation in special summer programs; and (5) other provisions that allow students extended learning experiences.

At the secondary school level, such provisions should be viewed as "vehicles" for providing differentiated learning experiences, not as the focus of differentiation. Too frequently, simply having an honors course or a mentor program is considered to be prima facie evidence that the needs of gifted students are being met. It is essential to examine the curricular structure of a provision and determine the degree to which differentiated learning experiences are being provided.

CONCLUSION

There is no such thing as a "gifted curriculum." There *are,* however, specific ways to modify the regular curriculum to increase the likelihood that learning experiences will be effective in developing the abilities of gifted students. Similarly, there is no such thing as "one best way" to manage programs for gifted students. The structure of the program must, however, support the development and the implementation of the differentiated learning experiences.

Classroom teachers hold a critical position in the education of all students, including those who are gifted. No program, whatever the curriculum and however it is managed, should "disenfranchise" the teacher in the regular classroom from providing services for gifted students.

The regular curriculum is composed of essential information and basic skills that should be mastered by all students, including the gifted. Therefore, the regular curriculum is appropriate for gifted learners. The regular curriculum is not, however, sufficient for helping gifted students develop and demonstrate their full potential. It is necessary to provide gifted students with "differentiated" learning experiences that will accommodate their different learning needs.

Our society, and all societies, are in part dependent on each individual having the opportunity to develop and use potentials in order to contribute her/his personal best. Without an admiration for and an encouragement of excellence, mediocrity becomes the goal of education. Minimal standards do not provide the foundation for a quality society. Opportunities for each student to achieve at a level commensurate with her/his potential allow a society of promise to become a society of productivity.

DISCUSSION QUESTIONS

1. In what ways are gifted students (in general) similar to and different from their age peers? How should these differences influence the structure and delivery of curricula for gifted learners?
2. What should be the role of the teacher in the regular classroom in providing services for gifted students? In what ways might administrators and others support teachers in their efforts?

3. How might teachers use curriculum as a means for identifying students who may be gifted? In what ways might teachers be able to recognize a "gifted response" by a student?
4. Identify and discuss specific services that are already provided to gifted students in your classroom or in your school. Given the information in the chapter, what are the strengths and shortcomings of existing services? How might the strong elements be maintained and the weak elements be modified?
5. Develop a list of information or materials that you would like to have in order to try some of the ideas in this chapter. Whom might you contact for support? Call or write the consultant for gifted education in your state department of education for suggestions.

REFERENCES

1. Borland, J. "Teacher Identification of the Gifted: A New Look." *Journal for the Education of the Gifted* 2 (1987): 22–32.
2. Clark, B. *Growing Up Gifted.* Columbus, Ohio: Merrill Publishing Co., 1988.
3. Curry, J. "Description of a Junior High School Program for the Gifted/Talented." In *Secondary Programs for the Gifted/Talented,* edited by Irving S. Sato. Ventura, Calif.: Ventura County Schools, 1981.
4. Curry, J., and Epley, T. "A Model for Establishing Continuity in Identification of the Gifted/Talented." In *Educating the Preschool/ Primary-Gifted and Talented,* edited by Sandra N. Kaplan. Ventura, Calif.: Ventura County Schools, 1980.
5. Gallagher, J. J. *Teaching the Gifted Child.* Boston: Allyn and Bacon, 1985.
6. Gear, G. "Effects of Training on Teachers' Accuracy in the Identification of Gifted Children." *Gifted Child Quarterly* 22 (1978): 90–97.
7. Kaplan, S. N. *Inservice Training Manual: Activities for Developing Curriculum for the Gifted/Talented.* Ventura, Calif.: Ventura County Schools, 1979.

8. Kaplan, S. N.; Madsen, S.; Gould, B.; Platow, J. A.; and Renzulli, J. S. *Inservice Training Manual: Activities for Identification/Program Planning for the Gifted/Talented.* Ventura, Calif.: Ventura County Schools, 1979.

9. Maker, C. J. *Curriculum Development for the Gifted.* Rockville, Md.: Aspen Systems Corp., 1982.

10. Parke, B. N. *Gifted Students in Regular Classrooms.* Boston: Allyn and Bacon, 1989.

11. Renzulli, J. S. *The Enrichment Triad Model: A Guide for Developing Defensible Programs for the Gifted and Talented.* Wethersfield, Conn.: Creative Learning Press, 1977.

12. Richert, E. S.; Alvino, J. J.; and McDonnel, R. C. *National Report on Identification: Assessment and Recommendations for Comprehensive Identification of Gifted and Talented Youth.* Sewell, N.J.: Educational Improvement Center, South, 1982.

13. Samara, J. "Independent Study Options for Able Learners." Unpublished presentation materials. Gorham, Maine: University of Southern Maine, Spring 1989.

14. VanTassel-Baska, J., and Strykowski, B. *An Identification Resource Guide on the Gifted and Talented.* Evanston, Ill.: Center for Talent Development, Northwestern University, 1986.

Chapter 9

MICROCOMPUTER APPLICATIONS FOR TEACHING STUDENTS WITH EXCEPTIONAL NEEDS IN THE REGULAR CLASSROOM

by Berttram Chiang

Berttram Chiang notes that in the 1990s, as the Regular Education Initiative is implemented, students with exceptional needs will not be pulled out of regular classes; instead, the most effective techniques available will be used to deliver services to them in regular class settings. As more teachers prepare to meet the challenge of working with students who are exceptional in regular classrooms, microcomputers will assume a greater role as an effective tool for instruction and management. Dr. Chiang discusses the uses of the microcomputer for teaching students with exceptional needs in regular classrooms.

As more and more teachers are preparing to meet the emerging challenge of working with students who are exceptional in regular classrooms, microcomputers are likely to assume an increasingly more important role as an effective and efficient tool for instruction and management. During the 1970s and the early 1980s, in the context of mainstreaming students with mild and moderate handicaps into regular classrooms, the resource room was the most popular service delivery model used by the schools to meet the needs of exceptional students. In the 1990s, with the implementation of the Regular Education Initiative (REI), which involves the restructuring of regular and special education for

163

students with exceptional needs, the emphasis will be shifted from pulling these students out of regular classes to utilizing the most effective techniques available to deliver services to them in regular class settings.

The microcomputer's capabilities as an effective instructional and management tool for students with exceptional needs have been widely recognized in the field. However, it is also important to realize that all students, including those who have no exceptional educational needs, can benefit substantially from appropriate microcomputer applications. In fact, a combination of these dual purposes—using microcomputers for both students with special needs and students without special needs—led Hagen to describe the microcomputer as a "common denominator" (20, p. 84) between regular and special education. This chapter acquaints the reader with (a) how to use microcomputers to maximize individualized instruction with students who are exceptional and (b) how to use microcomputers to manage a more diverse classroom.

THE MICROCOMPUTER AS A TOOL

Traditionally, teachers use a relatively limited set of tools to fulfill their role of imparting knowledge to students. Until the advent of microcomputers, technical tools required for teaching were exemplified by chalkboards, ditto duplicators, overhead projectors, film projectors, television, calculators, audio or video cassette recorders, and various laboratory equipment. As a teaching tool, microcomputer applications are unique in at least two aspects—power and versatility. The microcomputer is such a powerful tool that when its potential is fully realized it can dramatically change the classroom environment, the educational process, and teacher roles.

Unlike other educational tools, the microcomputer can serve multiple purposes. In addition to using it as instruction, teachers can use the microcomputer for a host of management functions. These include (a) motivating or reinforcing students; (b) monitoring student progress; (c) generating reports to communicate with parents and other professionals; (d) producing tests, worksheets, posters, and bulletin board materials; and (e) deciding whether a student should be referred for special education and other related services.

Since its arrival in our schools a few short years ago, teacher attitudes toward microcomputer use in the classroom have been mixed. They range from total embrace (i.e., computers are cure-alls) to complete rejection (i.e., computers will replace teachers) to wishful thinking (i.e., computers are just another fad). While changes of attitude toward this technology are gradual, most teachers do understand that the computer is only a medium that can be used to achieve the goal of individualized instruction. Morsink (31) has suggested that individualized instruction is a plan for organizing instruction rather than an instructional method per se. To the extent that individualized instruction is "the very essence of special education" (1, p. 109), microcomputers assume an important role for teachers who face the challenging task of teaching and managing special-needs students in mainstreamed classrooms.

THE MICROCOMPUTER AS AN INSTRUCTIONAL TOOL

The use of microcomputers provides students who are exceptional with more opportunities for appropriate practice and permits teachers to spend more instructional time with them (5). It should be emphasized, however, that careful planning and preparation are essential for microcomputer activities to maintain their instructional value and relevancy. Clearly, the integrity of microcomputer instruction would be seriously compromised if students were assigned to the computer just to be kept busy in order to free the teacher to do other tasks.

In the so-called "pullout" programs for students with mild handicaps, too much attention has been given to basic skill compensation at the expense of developing independent problem solving and critical thinking skills. While skill-building computer drill programs have been found beneficial in raising student achievement scores, particularly in arithmetic and to a lesser degree in language arts, simulation programs in social studies and science enable students to engage in discovery learning and higher-level cognitive skills. Additionally, Logo programs can provide ample opportunity for students to reflect upon their metacognitive processes. Word processing programs can offer a number of advantages in getting students to improve not only the product but also the process of writing. In order to function adequately in mainstreamed classes, students who are exceptional need to possess a minimum level of independent study and problem-solving skills. Microcomputer programs can be used to help students with exceptional needs improve their test-taking skills, error monitoring, self-questioning, and other task-specific learning strategies.

MICROCOMPUTERS AND RELUCTANT LEARNERS

Using graphic animation and arcade-type color and sound effects, microcomputers are generally very motivating for even the most reluctant students. We cannot assume, however, that the same programs can sustain their motivating power and popularity for an extended period of time. Unless teachers carefully delegate the game programs as reinforcement, contingent upon satisfactory performance in other academic and social areas, students are likely to lose interest in computer games once the initial curiosity wears off. For example, arrangements can be made so that students will earn a certain number of minutes of computer games by completing a specified amount of work. To maintain students' level of enthusiasm, it is also necessary to (a) exchange available software with other teachers periodically, and (b) expand the positive reinforcement associated with the computer games to other learning activities.

When students with exceptional needs who are in regular classes realize that they can be successful with computer games and other traditional computer programs and learning activities, they can become more self-confident and begin to develop a more positive attitude toward learning. There is evidence that students with learning disabilities become more attentive and less distracted when they are working with computers (37). The amount of positive social interaction and peer support has also been found greater when students with learning disabilities are learning Logo (10).

The motivational features of arcade-type computer programs include fantasy, curiosity, variable levels of challenge, clear-cut goals, fast pace, immediate feedback, and unlimited ceiling on performance (4, 15, 29). All these features are equally applicable to instructional effectiveness in general. Therefore, the most promising scenario is to integrate computer technology with effective instruction—that is, to use computers to "provide the foundation and catalyst for major changes in how instruction and learning take place in the public schools" (27, p. 175).

TEACHER ROLE CHANGES

How will the role of teachers be changed when the microcomputer becomes a more important source of information and learning tool in our schools? Gleason (17) suggests that when drill and practice of basic skills are handled by computers, teachers will be able to devote more time and energy to the teaching of higher-order objectives such as "social interaction, value development, civic responsibility, creative thinking and cultural appreciation" (p. 18).

167

In a mainstreamed class, planning and providing appropriate experience for students who are exceptional and their peers to interact with each other socially is especially important to the success of the Regular Education Initiative (REI). The emphasis placed upon social skill training that is made possible by having computers in the school is indeed an ironic counterargument against the notion that computers are dehumanizing. In fact, Weir (38), in a Computers in Classroom Instruction symposium, describes computers as "humanizers"— that is, as "an adjunct to socially mediated learning, as a part of a context, a constellation of children with children at the computer, of teachers with children with computers" (p. 61).

In his discussion of possible teacher role changes due to the introduction of new technology into our schools, Hawkridge (21) also suggests that the traditional dyad relation between the teacher and the class will be "transformed into a teacher-class-computer triangle" (p. 156). Instead of the traditional roles of imparting knowledge, evaluating student achievement, and maintaining discipline, teachers will be expected to engage in planning the computer use schedules, selecting and assigning courseware, monitoring interactions, and managing the flow of the class (21). In other words, students will be expected to be in more control of their learning "in appropriately structured computer-based environments" (38, p. 65). The benefit of achieving a sense of mastery and control for students with exceptional needs is critical for their own self-worth and acceptance by their peers.

To summarize, computers provide a mechanism to permit teachers to better attend to the individual needs of all students. The changes by no means imply that the teacher's role diminishes in significance. Nor do the changes suggest that a teacher's job is necessarily made easier. However, a creative teacher can take advantage of the computer as a teaching tool and make necessary adjustments to improve teaching so that all students can learn more.

STRATEGIES FOR COMPUTER APPLICATIONS WITH EXCEPTIONAL STUDENTS

For the computer to fulfill its roles in facilitating the Regular Education Initiative, a number of strategies need to be applied. These include (a) selecting quality software, (b) ensuring transfer of computer applications, (c) making adaptations and modifications for exceptional students, (d) integrating the microcomputer into the curriculum, and (e) encouraging cooperative learning with the computer.

Selecting Quality Software

The quality of instructional computer software has been improving noticeably. Many current programs, however, still reflect the problem of programmers' lack of familiarity with curriculum issues or educational theories and most teachers' insufficient understanding of programming. Consequently, many programs are fun but lack curricular relevancy and significance. For instance, a Hangman spelling program requires the student to randomly guess repetitively each letter for a correct spelling word. The only clue given is the number of letters in the spelling word. After six unsuccessful trials, the game is over with the completion of "the hanging." Another example of lack of consideration for instructional principles is shown in a program teaching the differentiation of cause and effect. When errors are made, a skier is wiped out, flips over, and falls. Since it is more exciting to see the skier flipping over than reaching the goal, the program actually reinforces the student's making error responses.

In addition to misuse or overuse of graphics, inappropriate use and control of sound effects was listed as one of the 10 commandments for rejecting instructional software (26). Fifty elementary school students using a word-matching computer program required fewer trials to complete the matching task under silent conditions than when a six-note music string repeatedly followed their responses (6). Judicious use of sound effects is particularly important for students with exceptional needs who usually have difficulties concentrating in the presence of auditory distractions. Audible responses that are associated only with error responses can also embarrass students with exceptional needs in the presence of their peers.

The reading level of the software and the ease of following directions on the screen are two other critical factors to consider when selecting computer programs for exceptional students. Many reference guides such as *The Yellow Book of Computer Products for Education, TESS: The Educational Software Selection, Only the Best: The Discriminating Software for Preschool to Grade 12,* and *Apple Computer Resources in Special Education and Rehabilitation,* as well as professional journals such as the *Journal of Learning Disabilities,* list and review current computer instructional programs. The best approach to selecting software for students with exceptional needs, however, is to preview the programs carefully to make sure that the students possess all the prerequisites to use the programs.

Ensuring Transfer of Computer Applications

Transferability of skills learned by computer is an important criterion, suggested by Hofmeister (23), when evaluating software programs. If the learning outcomes on the computer cannot be transferred to other situations, the value and benefit of the computer are obviously open to question. In a study by Chiang (7), fourth grade students with learning disabilities were found to be able to generalize their gains on multiplication skills from 12 days of drill and practice on computer to paper-and-pencil worksheet performance.

Degree of transfer from computers to other learning situations depends not only upon the specific software used. It also varies as the focus of the instructional software changes from learning simple information to concepts to rules to problem solving (24). Therefore, when transfer is less automatic in problem-solving situations from simulation software to real-life scenario, students who are exceptional need to be taught specifically to link the experience on the computer with the real world. In other words, instead of being the only avenue for learning a skill, the computer experience "must be embedded in other work with the same skill" (2, p. 139).

Making Adaptations and Modifications

In conjunction with the peripherals, microcomputers can be used to compensate for students' physical and sensory deficits (19, 33). For instance, keyboard modifications and speech recognition can open new worlds for students with physical disabilities. Voice synthesizers and other prosthetic devices can aid communication for students who are verbally impaired or mentally retarded. The Optacon Printing Reading System can be very useful for students with visual impairments, and the Telecaption Decoder helps students with hearing impairments.

In addition to making hardware adaptations by using various compensatory devices, it is necessary and desirable to modify software programs for students with exceptional needs in regular classes. Since most teachers are not interested in or capable of writing programs or even using authoring languages (e.g., PILOT, the BLOCKS, ASSIST) in order to develop instructional software, it is essential for prepackaged programs to have the capacity to be readily modified by teachers. Preferably, options should be available on the program menu to allow teachers to make various selections. For instance, the teacher should be able to choose the different levels of difficulty, the time allowed for each problem to be solved, the number of trials permitted, or the type of prompts and feedback needed. To individualize the program for students with exceptional needs, software should allow the teacher to add to the existing lessons different spelling words, vocabulary lists, and arithmetic facts.

It is an unfortunate fact that few programs are designed to allow the user to make modifications. In order to protect their program from being copied illegally, most programmers keep their program codes locked, thus making it impossible to see or change the codes. Among the few exceptions are the public domain programs, which can usually be modified.

Chiang (8) discussed 11 types of modification techniques that can be applied to enhance the quality of public domain instructional software. To illustrate the usefulness of program modifiability for students with exceptional needs, the program codes of the previously mentioned Hangman spelling program were changed to improve its flexibility and educational value. Instead of asking the student to randomly guess what the next letter is in a spelling word, the words were presented by categories such as "baseball words," "animal words," or "silent-e words." All the spelling words in a particular Hangman game were therefore related to a chosen category. The modified Hangman also allowed the teacher to create new categories of words or change words within any existing category. The category name appeared on the screen to serve as a clue. In addition, the direction on the screen included a reminder that the five vowel letters should be attempted first because every word contains at least one of those letters. Thus, the modified Hangman program guides the student to rely more on strategies than sheer luck.

Another example of program modification involves presentation of either single- or double-digit arithmetic facts, rather than both single- and double-digit facts, in a "math invader" program. In the original version of the program, students have to correctly answer a combination of arithmetic facts under time pressure; otherwise the descending alien invaders will destroy the earth. The modified version gives the student an option to choose arithmetic facts with or without regrouping. Such a modification is particularly necessary for students with exceptional needs who may not have learned a more advanced subskill (e.g., regrouping) but can benefit from the practice of a simpler subskill (e.g., adding single digits with a sum less than 10).

Integrating the Microcomputer into the Curriculum

Hofmeister (22) discussed the effect of microcomputers on instructional fragmentation. The use of microcomputers can "add to the complexity of the situation by introducing curriculum material out of sequence with the material of the regular classroom or the resource room" (p. 120). Careful coordination between regular and special education teachers can minimize such instructional fragmentations and promote congruence between software and curriculum content (32).

Since a majority of the current computer programs are not directly related to the curricular scope and sequence, computer applications are usually outside the context of overall curriculum and program development. Consequently, teachers are forced to use the microcomputer programs only as supplements to the regular curriculum. An example of a series of courseware that is more comprehensive is the Milliken Math Sequences. The program provides a sequential development of arithmetic skills including number readiness, addition, subtraction, multiplication, division, laws of arithmetic, integers, fractions, decimals, percents, equations, and measurement formulas. The program may be used for students from grades 1 through 8. Additionally, successful integration of the computer into the curriculum has to gain support of the school administration and requires preparation, cooperation, and communication among all staff at the district level, within the school building, and in each classroom (24).

Encouraging Cooperative Learning with the Computer

Although the student primarily interacts with the computer with no other peers involved, it should be pointed out that computer-assisted instructional activities are not bound to be isolated, individualistic interactions between students and the machine. In fact, many simulation and problem-solving computer software programs do lend themselves to a more productive learning style when two or three students as a team are assigned to one computer to work on the same problem. In contrast to a single learner interacting with the various situations in a program such as The Oregon Trail, the team approach generates a richer variety of social and collaborative interactions. Assigning two or three students to work at the computer at one time not only saves financial cost, but also provides opportunities for the students who are exceptional and their peers to learn and practice social skills such as turn taking, negotiating in decision making, and cooperation. For instance, students with exceptional needs and their peers can take turns editing each other's writing using word processing and spelling check programs (3). There is evidence that peer interactions in the Logo environment can facilitate social "behaviors that have cognitive underpinnings" (11, p. 100). These include conflict resolution, rule determination, and self-directed work.

Another advantage of cooperative learning with computer programs is that the teacher may match the peers in order to work together with a student who is exceptional and cannot read or use the keyboard properly. However, it is important for teachers to monitor the group interactions to ensure that no team member is overly dominant. Team members should also be changed periodically to maximize productive socialization.

In a study comparing learning-disabled and non-learning-disabled students who were learning Logo and on-task behavior (35), the two groups were paired to work at the computers. No significant differences were found between their knowledge of Logo functions. More importantly, their on-task behaviors did not differ. In a similar study (36), learning Logo at the computer in small groups was found to be more beneficial for students could share ideas and help group members. And in a study by Johnson, Johnson, and Stanne (25), the cooperative learning group was also found to be more goal-oriented and persistent than either the competitive or the individualistic group while using a simulation computer program.

Attitude change toward accepting students who are exceptional is critical to the success of implementing the Regular Education Initiative. This requires teachers to develop strategies for modifying stereotypic and negative attitudes toward students with exceptional needs (14). Hence, one of the most significant advantages of cooperative learning for students with exceptional needs is that "working together at the computer made subjects perceive their teammates more favorably" (30, p. 167). It is indeed exciting to envision the potential of involving microcomputer use as "an arena of collaboration and cooperation among regular and special education administrators, teachers and students" (18, p. 331).

THE MICROCOMPUTER AS A
MANAGEMENT TOOL

As students who are exceptional are fully integrated into regular classrooms, collaborations between regular and special educators will not be limited to just the delivery of instruction to these students. It is expected that much of the collaboration and consultation will center on initial referral, assessment, IEP development, and parent involvement. Computers can be used to minimize the record keeping and paperwork required for the sake of maintaining accountability. For example, computerized IEP programs can lead to data-based shared planning by regular and special educators on the one hand, and to more effective communications between teachers and parents on the other hand.

Other examples of computer technology use to facilitate decision making are through the use of expert systems to determine prereferral interventions (9), to provide a second opinion about placement decisions (12), to interpret test results (28), and to suggest strategies for diagnosing students' social-emotional behavior problems (13). An expert system uses the same interactive processes that consultants do and "replicates the expertise humans use to solve problems" (34, p. 2). To the extent that collaborative consultations are important in implementing the Regular Education Initiative, the development of expert system programs for teacher use is essential.

Other innovative uses of computers aimed at more effective use of teacher time include the generation of lesson plans, crossword puzzles, arithmetic fact sheets, customized parent reports, grade books, and readability checks and analysis. The exciting management possibilities of the microcomputer can be further expanded via an electronic bulletin by using modems. Access to on-line information systems such as SpecialNet, operated by the National Association of State Directors of Special Education, enables teachers to keep abreast of current remedial methods and materials, new diagnostic tests, conferences, workshops, publications, and other professional opportunities.

TIPS FOR TEACHERS

Throughout this chapter various suggestions have been made for teachers to use microcomputers for teaching students with exceptional needs in the regular classroom. The following list summarizes some practical tips for teachers.

1. Preview software programs carefully to make sure that students possess all the prerequisites to use the programs independently.
2. Write on index cards the step-by-step procedure for each software program and place the card within the floppy disk pocket. For general procedures or rules, make posters and display them near the computer area.
3. Use color codes to assist the student to distinguish some of the frequently used keys on the keyboard. For

instance, a green dot sticker may be glued on the "Return" or "Enter" key; a red dot sticker on the "Reset" key.

4. In addition to using the microcomputer as an instructional tool, make it a habit to use it to handle record keeping and other paperwork related to the student with exceptional needs. Your frequent use of the computer for such professional purposes sends an important message to students: computers are friendly tools for all of us.

5. Exchange software programs with other teachers. Coordinate with special education teachers with regard to selection and scheduling of computer programs and activities.

6. Assign two students of different skill levels to one cooperative team while using a word processing program to write and edit stories together. Have the printed stories displayed on bulletin boards or compile them into books. Integrating graphics or art work with such writing projects can make them even more rewarding.

CONCLUSION

In a recent article on the Regular Education Initiative, Gerber (16) eloquently articulated the intimate relationship of instructional tolerance modification and instructional technology implementation. As more students with exceptional needs are fully integrated in regular classrooms, teachers will inevitably be confronted with increased variability in student ability levels and learning styles. "Equal instructional time for each student will result in unequal outcomes" (16, p. 311). Given the dwindling budget, it is not realistic to expect significant increase in resource allocations and substantially reduced class size. Therefore, teachers have to rely upon more powerful technologies to have a reasonable chance to be effective with difficult-to-teach low achievers in the mainstreamed classes. In fact, if teachers can capitalize on the unique capabilities of the microcomputer, all students, including those with exceptional needs, will benefit from personalized instruction, which is a core component of effective teaching and the basic tenet of the Regular Education Initiative (39).

DISCUSSION QUESTIONS

1. Explain how teacher roles change in a microcomputer-based instructional environment.
2. Briefly discuss how microcomputer applications can be used to promote social interactions between students who are exceptional and their peers.
3. A common criticism of microcomputer applications is that they result in instructional fragmentation. Suggest procedures for ensuring that the microcomputer is appropriately integrated into the curriculum.
4. Give two reasons why software modifiability is desirable for microcomputer use by exceptional students.
5. Briefly describe some of the management activities that can be carried out by the microcomputer.

REFERENCES

1. Bennett, Randy E. "Applications of Microcomputer Technology to Special Education." *Exceptional Children* 49, no. 2 (1982): 106-13.
2. Budoff, Milton; Thormann, Joan; and Gras, Ann. *Microcomputers in Special Education.* Cambridge, Mass.: Brookline Books, 1984.
3. Bullough, R. V., and Beaty, L. F. *Classroom Applications of Microcomputers.* Columbus, Ohio: Merrill, 1987.
4. Chaffin, Jerry D.; Maxwell, Bill; and Thompson, Barbara. "ARC-ED Curriculum: The Application of Video Game Formats to Educational Software." *Exceptional Children* 49, no. 2 (1982): 173–79.

5. Chiang, Berttram. "Teaching Reading: A Review of Software." *Computers, Reading and Language Arts* 2, no. 2 (1984): 25–26.

6. _____ . "Overuse of Sound Effects in a Microcomputer Program and Its Impact on the Performance of Students with Learning Difficulties." In *Proceedings of the National Computer Conference for the Disabled,* edited by J. E. Roel, 55–59. Menominee, Wis.: University of Wisconsin-Stout, 1984.

7. _____ . "Initial Learning and Transfer Effects of Microcomputer Drills on LD Students' Multiplication Skills." *Learning Disability Quarterly* 9, no. 2 (1986): 118–23.

8. _____ . "Modifying Public Domain Software for Use by the Learning Disabled Student." *Journal of Learning Disabilities* 19, no. 5 (1986): 315–17.

9. _____ . "Special Education Referral Consultant: An Expert System for the Decision-Making of Pre-referral Interventions." Computer program. Oshkosh, Wis.: University of Wisconsin-Oshkosh, 1988.

10. Chiang, Berttram; Thorpe, Harold W.; and Lubke, Margaret. "LD Students Tackle the Logo Language." *Journal of Learning Disabilities* 17, no. 5 (1984): 303–4.

11. Clements, Douglas H., and Nastasi, Bonnie K. "Social and Cognitive Interactions in Educational Computer Environments." *American Educational Research Journal* 25, no. 1 (1988): 87–106.

12. Ferrara, Joseph M., and Hofmeister, Alan M. "CLASS.LD2: An Expert System for Classifying Learning Disabilities." Computer program. Logan, Utah: Utah State University, 1984.

13. Ferrara, Joseph M., and Serna, Richard. "Behavior Consultant: An Expert System for the Diagnosis of Social/Emotional Behavioral Problems." Computer program. Logan, Utah: Utah State University, 1985.

14. Fiedler, Craig R., and Simpson, Richard L. "Modifying the Attitudes of Nonhandicapped High School Students Toward Handicapped Peers." *Exceptional Children* 53, no. 4 (1987): 342–49.

15. Frederiksen, J.; Warren, B.; Gillote, H.; and Weaver, P. "The Name of the Game Is Literacy." *Classroom Computer News* (May/June 1982): 23–27.

16. Gerber, Michael M. "Tolerance and Technology of Instruction: Implications for Special Education Reform." *Exceptional Children* 54, no. 4 (1988): 309–14.

17. Gleason, Gerald T. "Microcomputers in Education: The State of the Art." *Educational Technology* 21, no. 3 (1981): 7–18.

18. Goldman, Susan R.; Semmel, Dorothy S.; Cosden, Merith A.; Gerber, Michael M.; and Semmel, Melvyn I. "Special Education Administrators' Policies and Practices on Microcomputer Acquisition, Allocation, and Access for Mildy Handicapped Children: Interface with Regular Education." *Exceptional Children* 53, no. 4 (1987): 330–39.

19. Green, John O. "New Ways for Special Ed Kids to Communicate." *Classroom Computer Learning* 5, no. 3 (1984): 24–29.

20. Hagen, Delores. *Microcomputer Resource Book for Special Education.* Reston, Va.: Reston Publishing Co., 1984.

21. Hawkridge, David. *New Information Technology in Education.* Baltimore: Johns Hopkins University Press, 1983.

22. Hofmeister, Alan M. "Microcomputers in Perspective." *Exceptional Children* 49, no. 2 (1982): 115–21.

23. _____. *Microcomputer Applications in the Classroom.* New York: Holt, Rinehart, and Winston, 1984.

24. Howie, Sherry H. *Reading, Writing, and Computer.* Needham Heights, Mass.: Allyn and Bacon, 1989.

25. Johnson, Roger T.; Johnson, David W.; and Stanne, Mary B. "Effects of Cooperative, Competitive, and Individualistic Goal Structures on Computer-assisted Instruction." *Journal of Educational Psychology* 77 (1985): 668–77.

26. Lathrop, Ann. "The Terrible Ten in Educational Programming." *Educational Computer* 2, no. 5 (1982): 34.

27. Lillie, David L.; Hannum, Wallace H.; and Stuck, Gary B. *Computers and Effective Instruction.* New York: Longman, 1989.

28. Lubke, Margaret M. "Math Test Interpreter: An Expert System for Interpreting Key Math Diagnostic Arithmetic Test." Computer program. Logan, Utah: Utah State University, 1985.

29. Malone, T. W. "What Makes Computer Games Fun?" *Byte* (December 1981): 258–77.

30. Mevarech, Zemira R.; Stern, Dafna; and Levita, Irit. "To Cooperate or Not to Cooperate in CAI: That Is the Question." *Journal of Educational Research* 80, no. 3 (1987): 164–67.

31. Morsink, Catherine V. *Teaching Special Needs Students in Regular Classrooms.* Boston: Little, Brown and Co., 1984.

32. Panyan, Marion V.; Hummel, Jeffrey; and Jackson, Lewis B. "The Integration of Technology in the Curriculum." *Journal of Special*

Education Technology 9, no. 2 (1988): 109–19.

33. Pollard, James P. "Adaptive Devices for Special Education: How Three Technological Devices Make Learning Easier for the Handicapped." *Electronic Learning* 3, no. 5 (1984): 44, 46.

34. Thorkildsen, Ron J.; Lubke, Margaret M.; Myette, Beverly M.; and Parry, James D. "Artificial Intelligence: Applications in Education." *Educational Research Quarterly* 10, no. 1 (1985–1986): 2–9.

35. Thorpe, Harold; Chiang, Berttram; and Lubke, Margaret M. "A Comparison of LD and Non-LD Students' Learning of LOGO and On-task Behavior." *Computers in the Schools* 3, no. 3 (1986): 63–69.

36. Webb, Noreen M. "Microcomputer Learning in Small Groups: Cognitive Requirements and Group Processes." *Journal of Educational Psychology* 76, no. 6 (1984): 1076–88.

37. Weir, Sylvia. *Cultivating Mind: A Logo Casebook.* New York: Harper and Row, 1987.

38. _____. "The Computer in Schools: Machine as Humanizer." *Harvard Educational Review* 59, no. 1 (1989): 61–73.

39. Will, Madeleine C. "Educating Children with Learning Problems: A Shared Responsibility." *Exceptional Children* 52, no. 5 (1986): 411–16.

THE CONTRIBUTORS

Berttram Chiang is Professor and Chairperson, Department of Special Education, University of Wisconsin-Oshkosh. His research interests focus on microcomputer applications, curriculum-based assessment, and instructional strategies for students with learning disabilities.

Libby G. Cohen is Professor of Special Education and a previous holder of the Walter E. Russell Endowed Chair in Philosophy and Education at the University of Southern Maine, Portland. Her research interests include assessment of students with special needs, adapting instruction to meet the needs of students, and ethical issues of special education.

James A. Curry is Associate Professor at the University of Southern Maine, Portland. He serves as President of the National Association for Gifted Children and as a member of the Association for the Gifted. As a former secondary teacher, he worked with gifted students in the regular classroom and through special programs.

Raymond M. Glass is Professor of Special Education and Associate Director, Center for Professional Development, at the University of Maine at Farmington. He has written widely in the area of teaching students with behavior disorders.

Charles M. Lyons is Associate Professor of Special Education at the University of Southern Maine, Portland, and Associate Clinical Professor in the Department of Community Health at Tufts University School of Medicine.

Joanne W. Putnam is Associate Professor of Special Education at the University of Montana. Her interests include teaching students with severe disabilities, cooperative learning, social integration, and mainstreaming.

Toni Rees began teaching deaf students in England. She is currently an Assistant Professor at the University of Southern Maine, Portland. She has been active in the deaf community and has recently developed sign language interpreter training opportunities in Maine. Dr. Rees is particularly interested in informing public school personnel and the hearing community about appropriate ways in which to work with deaf and hard-of-hearing individuals.

Loraine J. Spenciner is Assistant Professor at the University of Maine at Farmington. She has completed several investigative studies around the use of inner language and problem-solving strategies used by young children. She is also interested in the use of computer technology, assistive devices, and the integration of software into the curriculum of mainstreamed classrooms.

Jo Anna Spruill is Assistant Professor at the University of Wisconsin-Oshkosh. Her interests include the use of curriculum-based assessment with students with special needs and instructional strategies for adolescents with mild handicaps.

Susan B. Tarver is Coordinator for Training for the Teachers of Elementary Schools Program at the University of Southern Maine, Portland. As a consultant, she has assisted school districts and agencies in planning and implementing programs for gifted students. As a former elementary school teacher, she has worked with gifted students in the regular classroom and through resource programs.